C000090098

**REAL LIFE TIPS
FOR BLENDING YOUR BUNCH**

TIFFANY GRAVELLE

Copyright © 2020 by Tiffany Gravelle.

All rights reserved. No part of this publication may be reproduced,
distributed or transmitted in any form or by any means, including
photocopying, recording, or other electronic or mechanical
methods, without the prior written permission of the publisher,
except in the case of brief quotations embodied in critical reviews
and certain other noncommercial uses permitted by copyright law.
For permission requests, write to the author, at:

Tiffany Gravelle
www.blendednotstirredbook.com
hello@hellotiffany.com

Ordering Information:
Quantity sales. Special discounts are available on quantity
purchases by corporations, associations, and others. For details,
contact Tiffany Gravelle/hello@hellotiffany.com.

Blended Not Stirred/ Tiffany Gravelle. —1st ed.

Hardback ISBN: 978-1-7358060-0-6
Paperback ISBN: 978-1-7358060-1-3
E book ISBN: 978-1-7358060-2-0

Cover Photograph by Ruvim Noga on Unsplash

PRAISE FOR "BLENDED NOT STIRRED"

Anyone who has lived through the daunting task of blending two families can tell you it comes with challenges and triumphs you could never have anticipated. In this beautiful book the author captures both the highs and lows of blending in a heartfelt and hilarious recount of personal experiences. Her insightful and thoughtful approaches offer a great guide for a newly blended family and a nostalgic feeling of solidarity for those of us who have been there. A reminder that none of us are perfect but if your heart is in the right place and you're willing to try, you'll soon find yourself on the other side of your blended mountain.

Melanie Kagan, CEO, The Center for Family Resources
(Blended Mom of 5)

Tiffany Gravelle is the consummate expert on celebrating life and special occasions. She's brought that same joyous outlook to one of the hardest experiences to navigate – blending one family with another. Tiffany's vulnerable, honest look at her own mistakes and foibles as she faced these challenges and her hard-learned advice will help so many others find a multitude of ways to truly celebrate this new chapter of their life.

Lisa Abeyta, Founder, CityLife Inc.

"This is a must read for anyone who has a blended family, is thinking about blending families, or honestly… for anyone that has kids! Tiffany teaches lessons from the heart (and WTF lessons) based on her experiences. This book will make you question your own values and beliefs, and at the same time make you laugh out loud as you take a breath and realize how much her story connects to your own past. I love Tiffany's perseverance, tenacity, grit, and belief that love truly makes a family. She teaches us to be resilient and shine our light, even when all the strikes are against us."

Barbra Portzline, PhD, Founder, Organizational Rebel

DEDICATION

To my precious Brady Bunch who took me on the adventure of a lifetime. I love you and would not have it any other way.

To Mandi, my ride or die who had my back through every step and encouraged me to write it down.

FOREWORD FOR BLENDED NOT STIRRED

As a clinical psychologist who works exclusively with adults, I can attest that the woes and wins of the parenting journey make appearances on the therapeutic couch daily. Perhaps it is because we parents feel that parenting is our weightiest task and the greatest metric through which our legacy is assessed. Perhaps it is because the many moments in parenting can represent our greatest joys and our greatest sorrows. Perhaps it is attributable to the depth and veracity of love we have for our children. Or perhaps it is because kids are far better at taking up their space in the world (and our narratives) than over-polished adults.

The highs and lows of the parenting journey are undeniably present – even when both parents are in the home and both actively engaged in parenting. Imagine, then, the complexities introduced by blending families that have well-established personalities, habits, lifestyles, and customs. As a biological mom, a former foster mom, an adoptive mom of older kids, and a foster-adopt mom who actively engaged with bio families, I have navigated (and continue to navigate) my own blended family experience. With no guideposts to cling to, I had to learn on the fly when to flex and when to stand firm. More importantly, I had to learn by trial-and-error how to do both.

Tiffany's book, Blended Not Stirred, is an authentic and indispensable voice that will ring familiar to any parent who has ever navigated the sometimes murky, sometimes exhilarating waters of blended parenting. As a blended mom reading Blended Not Stirred, I felt a comforting camaraderie in getting to be a fly on the wall of the full spectrum of Tiffany's blended parenting journey. I sensed a familiar chest tightening when I read about her missteps, and I had an urge to hoist her onto the team's proverbial shoulders when I read about her moments of grace and inclusion. As a psychologist, I appreciated Tiffany's infusion of practical advice for blended parents who are at an earlier leg of the blended journey than she is. She is radioing back to warn you of the hazards and to tell you where to forage for nourishment. Tiffany's guidance is sound and provides important thematic values that can guide day to day blended parenting decisions.

Of all of the parents I have treated in my practice, 48% are parenting in blended families, 33% are parenting in non-blended families with both biological parents in the home, and 19% are single parents who are co-parenting with an ex. These parenting demographics in my practice are consistent with the growing numbers of families in the U.S. that are blended (Pew Research Center, 2015), which highlights the need for a comprehensive library of resources to support blended families in their efforts. Blended Not Stirred adds to this library from the wise vantage point of a blended mom who has earned her stripes and lived to tell the tale.

Joye L. Henrie, Ph.D.
Owner: Desert Wise
Co-founder: Spire Group
Albuquerque, New Mexico
2020

BLENDED NOT STIRRED

I'll never forget the moment over lunch when my boyfriend casually said to me "You know I've been thinking, we should move in together. What do you think?" Jaw drop. What? I was absolutely in love with him and we tried to spend every waking moment together. I already had a key. But moving in was, truthfully, not so simple. Between the two of us we had FIVE children. Five. One less than the Brady Bunch. What was that going to look like? There is absolutely nothing that could've prepared me for what came next.

This is my personal story of blending a family. I know there is no "one size fits all" solution for this. Some families struggle more than others, and for some, blending can be seamless. No matter what, families are always in flux with growing kids. There are always feelings to consider. Even more so when you are merging two (or more) families into one.

Our beginning was incredibly rough. My daughters missed their dad terribly (he moved out of state) and did not want to share me with anyone. This was true from the very start of dating my now husband, who was technically the first man to have even met my children post-divorce. I recall my oldest (10 at the time) convincing her little sister (7) to creep quietly behind the couches after their bedtime to spy on us. Big sister scared the bejesus out of her baby sister, convincing her there were burglars and murderers outside, causing her to burst into the living room hysterical and sobbing, begging someone to go look outside. And the worst incident – my oldest standing in the living room of our tiny townhouse screaming and trembling with rage in her oversized night shirt telling my boyfriend to "Get out! We don't want you here! I hate you! Stay away from my mom!" He handled that incident beautifully, speaking in a compassionate, low, calm voice, he tried to assure her that he was not going to take me away. I was sure we were headed for a break up. Then he told me "No ten-year-old angry girl is going to keep me away from you." Be careful what you wish for.

On the other hand, I thought I had started off on the right foot with my now step-kids. It turned out I was very wrong. The oldest daughter (8) would become incensed and shut down over things I never understood, and demand that she needed personal space. (There was not a lot of that in our house.) She would wrap herself into her tiny bathrobe and run and hide. They would not eat my food and kept secret stashes of junk food hidden under pillows and in closets. I was positive they were telling their mom what terrible people my daughters and I were when they got home from staying with us. (Found out later that this was in fact true.) My stepson went through a period (from about ages 7-10) where he refused to come over or speak to us. My husband would go to pick up his kids for the weekend and they would not get in the car. His ex's new husband even called him one day to "give him advice" on how to handle his kids. (Do not EVER do that by the way. Leave the parenting to the parents please.)

I felt extremely isolated in this new role, like I had no one to talk to that would understand what we were going through. Friends that had no children were dumbfounded and confused at our circumstances. Friends with kids were often judgmental and could not relate to our situation or methods. If I vented about my partner, my kids, or my step-kids, my friends became defensive of my feelings, but often said things that hurt more than helped. Initially we had serious opposition from more toxic friends, who are no longer in our life. While people were trying to be helpful, their well-meaning advice did not resonate to our experience. I would feel defensive about protecting my blended family and even more isolated than before.

After eight long years, many tearful nights, some yelling at our kids and each other, it is nothing like that anymore. It is bittersweet to remember what happened. My oldest daughter now adores her stepdad. She was maid of honor and gave the most beautiful speech at our wedding, thanking him for his parenting, love, and support in her hardest years. They enjoy each other's company and text and talk several times a week while she is away at college. They have a loving relationship, completely independent of mine.

My youngest daughter still butts heads with her stepdad frequently, but she loves him completely. He taught her how to ride a bike and snowboard, and he gave her his fancy camera when she was taking photography classes. He has shown up for her in every way possible – games, teacher conferences, art shows, dances, sports. While these two seriously still drive me crazy when they bicker, they are more alike than they realize.

My stepson moved in with us full time a couple of years ago, a miracle I never thought would happen! He is funny and loving, always making us laugh, eager to build or repair anything I need, and so very different from his sisters. Although his moving-in process was not smooth nor easy, I cannot imagine him being anywhere else. We miss his twin sister as she still lives full-time with her mom. She is a feisty, independent young woman, with a great sense of fun, who gives the most extraordinary full-body hugs on the planet.

My oldest stepdaughter is an incredible woman. We have found so much common ground over the years (we are very much alike) and we have bonded over our passion for books, her pursuit of education, and her laid back open-minded positive view on life. She is hardworking, sweet, and generous. As she got older, we have been able to have healing and very adult conversations on what our family has gone through, and what she experienced. She shared so much insight with me, and I have a better perspective and understanding.

All our kids love each other, want to spend time together, set dates to meet up independently, and text or Snapchat constantly. Over time, they came together and created their own unique bond. (This certainly did not happen overnight.)

My husband and I both have very cordial relationships with our ex-spouses, which has also been built over time. It has gone from very tenuous conversations, threats, and accusations to true co-parenting partnerships. We talk frequently to both and communicate what is going on with the kids, everything from events, to health, to behavior, to expenses. We celebrate milestone events and some holidays together and can hang out as friends. It is a game changer if you can do this for your kids.

Of course, there are still parenting challenges now and then. We are all learning and growing every day, but I believe we have found our groove. We cherish our time together and miss each other when we are apart. We feel most complete when we are all in the same room. We share a loving and authentic home. I am madly in love with each one of them, and I am incredibly grateful for what we have found.

Blending a family was my most intense, most heartbreaking, hair-tearing, super stressful, hardest, brain-melting multitasking job I have ever had. And, you don't get to clock out. Some days I am shocked we made it through. Some days I cringe when I think of how I could have done it better.

I want to give you hope. You are not on your own.

I am going to share with you examples of specific challenges our family faced, what lessons we learned, and some challenging feelings to consider. Whether you are blending a family of any kind, or just in a challenging family transition, I want to share my best tips and advice with you. I am not a doctor, and I am not perfect. I am a regular mom that experienced pain, growth, and an expansion of my heart that I did not know was possible when blending our family.

No matter what you take away from this book, I want you to remember that "Love Makes a Family." Different genders, colors, ages, personalities, parents, and kids. Make it a priority to create a loving safe space in your home. Stay consistent, have compassion, be humble, be honest, be kind. **And do not ever give up, even on your hardest day.**

YOURS, MINE AND OURS

This is a challenge I have discussed with my husband multiple times and it occurs on many levels. Stepparent to kids, parent to parent, kids to kids, exes and kids, exes and exes... there will be an ally to side with in any situation. Here are a few examples of what I am talking about.

You truly do not understand, nor have a biological heartfelt connection to the other person's children. That is normal. They will have personality traits, communication styles, and nuances like their individual parents. Things they do or say may grate on you in a way in which you have less patience and are quicker to lose your temper. In fact, if your own kids did the exact same thing, you may not even notice it, or you forgive faster.

The kids team up with their bio parent. It is an "us–versus–them" kind of situation. "Why don't you like my mom's muffins? Everyone likes them. What's wrong with you and why are you so mean?" Or, "Don't yell at my mom/dad! Leave them alone." Or, "You're not my parent, this is none of your business and I don't have to ask/tell you."

The ex-spouse calls or texts you. "I just spoke with our child and they told me...What exactly is going on in that house?"

Or the kids say, "In my family we used to...and it's way better than this." Or, "I hate you." Or, "Leave my sister/brother alone." Or, "I really miss my mom/dad/pet...I want to go/ move back there." Or, "I like them (the other parent) better than you." (Ouch.)

Sigh. This is the time where you really must get humble, swallow your pride, and check in with both your actions and communication. Determine what version of yourself you are sharing with your family. Personal ego often is in the driver's seat in a semi-truck loaded with emotions.

Then, you get to practice calm communication skills with non-shaming language to everyone involved. And if you need to take a hot minute to calm down? Do it. Go to your room, scream in a pillow, splash some water on your face and get back in there, champ! You will do this repeatedly. And then one hundred million more times.

Did you know a child's auditory processing skills do not develop until around 15 years old? That means they may have heard you say 'something,' but they are still processing the information. Going between households, parenting styles, rules, beds, friends, family, and pets is a hell of a lot of information to take in.

The University of Rochester Medical Center says this, "The rational part of a teen's brain isn't fully developed and won't be until age 25 or so. In fact, recent research has found that adult and teen brains work differently. Adults think with the prefrontal cortex, the brain's rational part. This is the part of the brain that responds to situations with good judgment and an awareness of long-term consequences. Teens process information with the amygdala. This is the emotional part. In teens' brains, the connections between the emotional part of the brain and the decision-making center are still developing—and not always at the same rate. That's why when teens have overwhelming emotional input, they can't explain later what they were thinking. They weren't thinking as much as they were feeling."

Yep, that hits the nail on the head.

Children love their biological parents. It is a bond that can not be broken. They will do anything to 'protect' the other parent to make them feel as though they aren't taking sides, including lying or misconstruing facts. They will dislike the new spouse because they think that is what their other parent wants and will work to seek favor. They will listen in on your conversations, peek at your text messages, and constantly monitor your feelings to interpret what they should absorb throughout the divorce and hold grudges that do not belong to them. They will desire the absent parent, idolizing them in their absence. They will start acting like a tiny adult taking on tasks that should never belong to a child or revert to babyish behavior, asking to sleep in bed with you, throwing tantrums, or having accidents. You may get to be the parent that hands out the carrot sticks and punishments, while the other parent is always Disneyland and hot fudge sundaes.

Lesson Learned
· · · · · · · · · · · · · · · · · ·

My husband and I have always been committed to consistency in our home. The default trick we used when we were most angry was to find one singular positive attribute about the kid driving us crazy and focus on it. Even if it was as small as a minor physical trait, "They look great in the color green." Or something more substantial, "They really love their siblings and can speak up for them." That method helped us recognize the good in that kid and redirect our energy. Love first. Love always.

Now that we are better blended, it is much easier to recognize how incredible and unique each child is and appreciate them for who and what they are. It is really freaking hard to do when they are coming at you in a tornado of high emotions, teeth, and tears. Here is the thing. They have always been awesome, and anger is a nasty veil that blocks your view. When my husband and I say or write our daily gratitude, each child is listed individually with their many positive qualities, and it helps to remember them on the hard days.

Another time, my oldest daughter was writing a middle

school assignment on "who she most admired." I was gutted to see it was about her bio dad. I was still reeling with fresh divorced feelings of "He moved away, he's not here to do anything we need. He is missing everything important in your life and we're here every day doing the hard work. He's your hero and you hate us?" Combined with her constant reminders of how unhappy she was and how much she hated my partner; it was hurtful to both of us.

In her developing teen brain, she was really missing her dad and elevating him to a significant place of importance in her life. It was easy to idolize the absent parent that was always loving and fun, and to blame the ones that were creating structure and rules and causing her perceived unhappiness.

Challenging Feelings to Consider

Obviously remembering brain and emotional development, keep in mind that the feelings the children are expressing are true to them at the time. Make room, but do not engage or encourage destructive behavior. Give everyone time to calm down and speak without yelling. Start an open conversation and ask leading questions. "Tell me more about that" is a favorite of mine.

When you take opposition to your spouse, it creates a

greater divide. Have those adult conversations in private, keeping an open mind and heart. Do not weaponize your words. Do not demonize your partners children and compare them to your own. You parents are on the same team and need to provide a united, calm, consistent front. The stepparent needs to provide a supporting role to the bio parent, and vice versa. Have each other's backs. One of the best things we did as blended parents was to take a parenting class together called the Nurtured Heart Approach ®. If a facilitated class is not available near you, check out the book **Transforming the Difficult Child** *by Howard Glasser.*

THIS HURTS ME...

This is a non-negotiable discussion to have with your new partner. I promise there are so many variables around this topic you should write them down for sanity's sake. Discuss your core values and expectations for the family, the earlier the better. Are you on a strict schedule or are Dad's weekends more like a mini vacation? Do the children have to eat what is served or can they choose an alternative? What are the curfews? What chores are expected? What parenting rules did you and your former spouse agree on? And the mega monster – which parent dishes out discipline to which children? Are you supposed to get involved? My hot tip for the last question – the parent of the child in question should issue the discipline as a united front with the other partner, even if they live with you full time.

Additionally, talk often about permissions and rules with your partner. Kids may use this opportunity to ask for something from one of you if they know the other will say no (or they may already have.) This goes especially with your ex-spouse. Keep the communication consistent.

Ask the kids for input on house rules and expectations. They will better understand why the rule is in place and what the consequence is for breaking it. Ask them what an appropriate consequence might look like. Keep it reasonable, and let the punishment fit the crime. Do not waiver on the consequences. Ever. Remember the "this hurts me more than it hurts you" statement? Well, it does. Especially when you have to cancel a much-needed overdue happy hour with your girlfriends to play 'the bad guy.'

Post the rules in a common family area for all to see. If a rule needs adjusted, great! Do it before it is broken. And finally, kids will break the rules, and sometimes break your heart. Be sure to criticize the ACTION of breaking the rule, but not the kiddo. They need to know you love them unconditionally, but they broke trust.

Here is one of my favorite resources in creating your guidelines of discipline in a blended household.

The 5 C's of Effective Discipline: Setting Rules for Children, by Ben Martin, Psy.D.

CLARITY: Be clear when you set rights, rules, and limits.

CONSISTENCY: Be consistent in enforcing rules.

COMMUNICATION: Talk about rights, rules, and limits often.

CARING: Use encouragement and support, not just discipline for broken rules. Recognize when things go right!

CREATE: Instill a sense of social responsibility in your children.

Lesson Learned
• • • • • • • • • • • • • • • • • •

After working a 15-hour day, I got home very late, opened an adult beverage, and kicked up my feet next to my husband on our couch. Not five minutes later, I got a frantic call from my youngest daughter who was a junior in high school at the time. She had been arrested at a nearby neighborhood park for drinking alcohol and she was drunk. Here's the kicker – all of her "friends" had left her ALONE after 11:00 pm in a pitch-dark park with bottles of booze. (WHAT?!) It was her birthday weekend. She had gone out with permission and was planning to spend the night at her friend's. The officer gets on the phone and tells me he will hold her without charges if I come to pick her up. After hanging up, I yell and curse and jump in the car. En route, the officer calls me back to say her "friends" came back, appear to be sober, so he is releasing her to them. Another mental explosion (NO!) I go straight to the friend's house and wait for them to arrive. I quickly text my husband to let him know we are all safe. Then, I call my ex-husband to fill him in and have him wait on the phone with me until she gets in the car. I am immensely grateful to my ex (who lives out of state) for co-parenting with me that night. I am also deeply thankful for my sweet husband for not criticizing the discipline choices we made for her and staying calm and supportive through all of it. Including the very unpleasant aftermath of long-term enforcement of consequences. I am proud to say my daughter worked extremely hard to earn back our trust by demonstrating responsibility in many ways over time and has trusted me with private information and decisions since then.

My favorite house rule is that we do not allow our kids to spend the night with friends anymore. Their friends are more than welcome to stay here. This is for their safety and my peace of mind. We make sure we have tons of snacks and drinks on hand, and lots of fun things to do. After the initial shock of that rule from the kids, it has saved us so much headache and heartache. Except for the time my oldest daughter's friend snuck a liter of sour green apple vodka into the house and they drank it all... that was a bad couple of days. My daughter still cannot smell or taste green apple to this day without gagging. I saved the bottle. I plan on putting a commemorative plaque on it and lovingly passing it on to her as a baby shower gift someday.

Household chores was another sensitive subject. While one set of kids lived with us full time and had a rotating chore chart (we did not give allowance, but everyone could earn special treats or experiences) the other kids would come for the weekend and blaze a trail of sticky mess behind them causing irritation for both parents and kids. One of my pettiest moments (and sadly I had many) was when one of the visiting girls left a pile of destruction in the kitchen and departed without cleaning. On her next visit I purposely left out a similar disarray. When she saw it, she critically said "What's up with that mess?" to which I wickedly replied, "Oh, like the exact one you left last weekend?" She stormed out. There are so many ways I could have handled that one better, but I think I made a point. Cringe.

What our family settled on for chores was that the full-time kids stuck to their chore chart. Our part time kids helped set the table, clear dishes, and put them in the dishwasher, feed the dogs, and a few other easy items while they were with us. Happily, we have settled into a consistent groove of every kid, no matter when they are with us, chipping in to help and pairing up to help us out usually without us asking. It's seriously the best.

Challenging Feelings to Consider
. . . .

Some of the children will be with you only part time, every other weekend, or only during holidays or vacations. You will not be able to alter or adjust their normal behavior in 48 hours. Meaning, they will have a hard time following your rules. Choose your battles. Stay consistent. Talk to the kids and respect their privacy. It is worth building long term trust so they will come to you with their thoughts, opinions, and challenges.

feb ? 2013
Lexi G

I love the way
my house looks at dads

_____

THE RED SLEEPING BAG

At the beginning, living arrangements were tough for our family. We were merging two sisters that are almost three years apart, with my spouse's oldest daughter that is the same age as the youngest sister, and a set of twins, one boy and one girl who were inseparable, into our four-bedroom house. Ages 11, 8, 8, 6, and 6. Easy, you think, right? Put two sets of each sisters in a room and the last room for the boy. Nope. Over six years, we shuffled everything from the actual rooms, to bunk beds and futons, to single beds and queen beds, and even created an extra bedroom in the sunroom. We painted, we organized, we acquired special bedding and decorative items so that each kid had "their space" multiple times. And, as the kids grew older, it became more important for some of them to have their own rooms due to age or gender differences.

Lesson Learned

· · · · · · · · · · · · · · · · · ·

One of the kids was sleeping in a red sleeping bag on a futon when I moved in. In trying to create the new spaces, I packed up the sleeping bag and moved it with our camping gear in the garage and traded the futon for a twin bed with new bedding. Catastrophe! She loved that sleeping bag and was furious that I had taken it away. I also allowed other kids to use the sleeping bag on other occasions. Another angry moment. Here's the deal. She was eight, I was still a stranger, and I moved something very important and comforting to her without understanding the feelings or background of the item. It was "hers" at her dad's house and I took it away. When you are preparing to move and merge, you, your spouse, and your kids should do a quick inventory of important "must have" items in their space. Prepare them for the changes to the space and let them keep a top three or a top five very special items. Ask them for suggestions. Do I really care if she sleeps in a sleeping bag? NO! I just want all of my kids to sleep. But in trying to make it "homey" to me, I made it less-so for her.

Another gut-wrenching moment for me was when this same daughter brought over her own set of sheets and pillows for the bed. She said the ones we had were scratchy and she hated sleeping in them. My feelings and pride were hurt, and I was sad she did not tell me directly. But that's the thing. It was all pride and ego driving those feelings. In retrospect, I am so glad she brought something over that was her own and made her comfortable. I am thankful to her mom for shopping and getting her something she really loved to have at our home that made her stay more pleasant and comfy. When you are trying your best and your feelings get hurt, ask yourself, where it is truly coming from? Did someone intentionally work to hurt you with malice? Most likely not. Let that shit go.

Challenging Feelings to Consider

One set of kids might be making this their full-time home, with no second home to go to. The other set of kids may live mostly with the other parent, and it is imperative to make this home feel like theirs as well, so they enjoy staying and look forward to coming over. Be equal and be consistent about their personal items and space as much as possible, but give the full time kids a little extra compassion in their environment. It helped to create a "private space" in our overflowing home for any of the kids to take a time out when they needed it. It included a cozy chair next to some books with headphones and some glitter wands and small games designed to relax the participant. The others were told to let them have their peace. Fortunately, we never had to take turns.

By the way, we continued to play musical rooms right up until the oldest girls started to leave for college.

Kennedy taryn   2-26-15

we made a puzzle and glued it
together.

HEY, THAT'S MINE!

Ugh, this is something I look back on and think, "you dummy!" But I was truly thinking about simplicity and ease in putting five kids together in the same house. My Pollyanna dream was, "Hey Brady Bunch, let's all share!" Here is what I know now. There are family games and toys like DVDs, board games, coloring books, art supplies, Frisbees, basketballs, or bubbles. You get it. And then, there are private toys not to be touched or shared without permission. Like, if you buy an Easy Bake Oven, or a My Little Pony Dream Barn, or even a Nerf gun, you cannot expect that child to have any desire to share that toy with their sibling. It always depends on the day of course, but here are the rules that worked for us. Each kid had their personal toys and games separated into a bin and they were always off limits, unless that child was present, and you were invited to share. Obviously, we always encouraged sharing and playing together, but we allowed each child to keep between one to three toys private and inaccessible to others. They had to use kind words to their siblings, or they would lose privileges. Example: "May I share?" "No thank you, I'd rather play by myself." Once they laid claim, we supported their decision by telling the other kids to find another object of desire. Occasionally if something was so popular (as was common in our close-aged brood) we would buy a duplicate toy so that easy group-play could take place.

Separate bins and/or boxes were also kept for individual accessories, makeup, grooming items, cash money, special pens, rocks, slime, trinkets – whatever was precious to them, they just had to put it in the box. As they grew, bathroom drawers and shelves were labeled to help separate the goods. This did not stop the occasional swipe or borrow of perfume, moisturizer, or earrings.

When it is time to clean out the said boxes, the kids went through their individual items with us to keep, toss, and donate. There were occasional hand me downs, like the beloved Twilight posters that went from one girls' bedroom wall to the next, but overall, the kids became very adept at getting rid of the old.

Lesson Learned
. . . .

My doe-eyed optimism also led to a major clothing mistake. With girls the same ages and sizes I thought some clothing items could be shared. WRONG. Not only did every girl have a completely different style and taste, but if a favorite shared shirt was stained, ripped, or damaged in any way, all hell broke loose. It was definitely best practice to keep separate clothing items for each kid, and to allow for occasional hand-me-downs, which were never forced on the younger sibling.

If a big special occasion is coming up like school picture day, a party, wedding, or funeral, you have two options.

1) Speak with your ex-partner about a specific outfit that should be worn and make sure the proper parent has it in advance for the occasion.

2) Buy a full set of whatever you may need from shoes, to tights, to ties, and keep it ready in the closet.

Also remember that your spouse may want to keep a fully stocked closet for the traveling kids for ease of overnights, travel, and comforts of home. This was a hard one for me as we often had several items of never worn clothes with tags on that were quickly outgrown. "Why can't they just pack a bag?" is not an argument worth having. As the kids got older, the closets shrank. Now several pairs of pajamas, underwear, and socks are mostly what live here, and they do pack a bag of favorite items to go back and forth. They each still have their own shelves and boxes.

Challenging Feelings to Consider

. . . .

Keep in mind that items may travel from house to house. That super cool toy you bought them, or brand-name, ultra-fabulous sneakers may not ever make it back home. Kids may show up without underwear, or a toothbrush, or in something that does not fit. Do not sweat it. This stuff happens in non- blended families. No one is trying to undermine you. Your job is to create a comfortable and loving home for EVERYONE in the house and make coming and going as pleasant as possible.

9/7/13   Kennedy
I got to eat
waffels

WHO'S HUNGRY?

I will never forget the first family meal we had when we moved in. I made homemade chicken nuggets, mashed potatoes, and green beans. What kid wouldn't like that? (You may have just said "Mine!")

I juggled meal preparation in an unfamiliar kitchen and accidentally put a plastic serving spoon on the coiled electric burner. It started to smoke and melt. I quickly grabbed for it without thinking and burned the crap out of my hand. Holding back my tears while I held my hand underwater, I thought this was not getting off to a good start.

As I placed the dishes on the table three of the five kid's faces turned to disgust. "Ewww, what is that?" and "Ewww, I don't eat that." and "I'm not hungry." echoed from the table. I was instantly offended, and my kids were too (us-versus-them.) "What's wrong with my mom's food?!" I came from the school of 'eat what you are served,' but this was not the case in their family. I did not have picky eaters, I did not know picky eaters, and I did not know how to handle this one. We were recovering divorcees with five kids to feed and a tight budget. I was doing my best.

This family challenge took a very long time to manage and caused many arguments. I found two-liter sodas hidden in the closet and an array of candy and sweets stashed under pillows. There were calls to my partner saying that the kids were coming home starving and miserable. My partner weakly suggested we just order pizza instead, but only cheese and half with no sauce, and nothing green on the table. Or, he offered to make a watery mac and cheese and hot dogs (which I found disgusting) but would definitely be eaten. He was really trying too.

Lesson Learned
· · · · · · · · · · · · · · · · · ·

Step one: Find out what the kids do like to eat and make your best, healthiest version of that. One will only eat plain noodles with butter? Great! Make a batch of spaghetti for the family with meatballs and sauce on the side (for those that like it) and serve cut up veggies with ranch. (Extra points for having them help you cook. They are more likely to eat it!)

Step two: Keep exposing them to new foods and ask them to try what my family called 'scouts bites.' One small spoonful on their plates to taste. Did they happen to try something new at a friend's house that they enjoyed? Hooray! Duplicate.

Step three: Get them plastic boxes with sealable lids to stash their goods. I explained to them that when living in the high desert we are susceptible to mice and other vermin (insert your icky bugs here) that want to eat that candy, and it should be saved for after dinner.

Step four: Make a snack shelf with lots of healthy options and some junk, that the kids can access and enjoy at any time.

Step five: Check yourself before you wreck yourself. Give yourself some empathy and a pat on the back for providing delicious hot meals for your family. Or delicious hot take out. Or cold leftovers. Or packaged snacks. You are providing food. They will eat when they are hungry. Period.

Challenging Feelings to Consider

Food is love. Food is comfort. Food is family-culture. Do you spend time creating a must have side dish to complete your Thanksgiving every year? Do you long for your mom's grilled cheese with the crusts cut off? When you are sick with a cold do you crave chicken noodle soup, or pho, or baked beans on toast? Food has feelings around it. Your step-kids will most definitely have their most favorite and special foods that you are not familiar with, find disgusting, or do not understand. Who cares! Feed those little faces and start some table conversations with your family.

Brad   12-31-2012

I feel good that I
have my family together
to share the holidays with
me. Tiff, Taitum, Talyn, Lexi, Kenny
                        & Braden

HO-HO HOLIDAYS

Of all the many topics to cover during divorce, I think this is the cruelest, and I've yet to see the divorce decree parenting plan followed in this area. Sometimes parents move, or remarry, or special plans arise like trips or extended family gatherings. It is a unique challenge in a blended family.

Start discussing the holiday or birthday in question with your ex-partner in advance. Understand that in most cases both parents want to celebrate in some way with their child. Know that both of you trying to celebrate on the "actual day" is an exhausting nightmare waiting to happen. This is where the parenting plan comes in handy. What did you originally agree upon? Rotation of every other holiday on the calendar? Did you get even years or odd years? Try to stick with it. Have the grace to speak up in a civil manner if the first agreement does not work for you or the kids. Using a mediator whenever possible to update the agreement is less expensive and more pleasant than going back to the mattress with the lawyers. In short, don't be a selfish dick.

Holidays and birthdays are not the time to "one up" your ex by making better plans or buying better gifts. The best gift you can give your child is your undivided time and attention. Discuss your ex-partner's choices of gifts and plans in advance and play nice. In blending five children, it was imperative for us to set a budget with our gifts and stick to it consistently and equally. Not to mention the knowledge that our kids each still received gifts from their extended relatives on multiple sides of the family, and no less than four to five Christmas stockings each year. It has been important for us to tone it down and focus on less material things. I know this may not always be the case in every family. In our family, one ex-spouse has been great at communicating and matching our budget style and gift plans. The other's love language is gifts and they have the ability and desire for over the top expensive items that we cannot and will not compete with. In that case we always admire and positively comment on the kid's new treasures, and try to meet jealousy head on with the bio parent of the other children having a private discussion to recap our family priorities and how much they are loved by everyone regardless of gifts. We remind them how important it is to give rather than receive, which gave us another opportunity to create NEW traditions with our blended family.

My best example of creating new family traditions is Christmas. Trust me, we have created new traditions and family experiences for every holiday imaginable. But Christmas for us is typically very anticipated, precious, memorable, and family-centric. I am aware that what I am going to describe sounds intense, but with careful planning it has worked most of the time for five kids, four parents, and extended families with some located out of town.

During the month of December (year-round actually) we talk to the kids about people in need, the importance of giving, and collectively choose a few charities to support and a few giving activities. Together we have written love notes, created care packages for soldiers overseas, paid off lay-aways at local stores, handed out warm wool socks to the homeless, paid for people's drinks, food or groceries, sponsored gifts for needy families and children, served food, and a few others. That way, we demonstrate the importance of being a caring and active citizen, helping our community, and giving what we can as a family. The time we get to spend together doing it is pretty fantastic too.

We also make sure that our kids can attend extended family parties whenever possible. I have dropped off my girls at my ex-husband's family party almost every year with gifts and treats to share. Because he is out of town, it is especially important for them to stay connected.

Typically, around December 23, we have a special, very formal "Nutcracker" tea with my parents, followed by "The Nutcracker" ballet at a historic theater Downtown. My mom goes all out with different themed table settings and incredible food every year. This is their gift to us, and all the kids love it. Following that, we parents race home and send the kids out together for hot chocolate and to look at lights. This obviously became MUCH easier as when they started driving. Following one of the spectacular moments in the Disney

'Nutcracker' movie, we create a string maze that leads to a small gift. We assign each kid a color of yarn and weave an elaborate maze up and down and around, low, and high throughout the house and yard. The maze gets more difficult as they get older. Each year the gift at the end of the string is matching Christmas pajamas. They run upstairs to change, we open some Christmas crackers, wear the paper crowns, tell jokes, play with the tiny toys, and talk about the day. Sometimes they get to open one gift and head to bed.

December 24th is our "Christmas" which starts with stockings and breakfast, moves to opening gifts (taking turns and rotating) and ends with a simple holiday dinner. The food is great, but we keep it casual. Then one set of kids leaves for the other parent's home to wake up Christmas day. This was outlined in the divorce parenting plan.

December 26th we rotated between "Boxing Day" and stockings at my parent's house, and driving out of town to see another set of grandparents, aunts, uncles, and cousins to celebrate Christmas again with all of the kids, or my girls heading to their dad's. This may rotate or change each year depending on kids' schedules and family arrangements.

Lesson Learned
. . . .

This could also be classified under challenging feelings, but as we are also making some accommodations this coming year, I consider it a lesson. As I described, our Christmas Day is December 24th and on December 25th we typically relax. We stay in pajamas, make delicious food, watch movies, play with gifts, call family, and only really leave the house at night to see the luminaria tour Downtown. This last year my daughters were very upset on Christmas Day. They shared that they felt cheated that their step siblings got to go to another house and celebrate all over again while they were forced to celebrate early and only once. They were mad that their dad lived out of state and they felt cheated of a "normal" Christmas Day. While I was frustrated hearing this after making extensive plans to accommodate everyone, I do not think their feedback is selfish. It is not about the gifts. It is about them feeling different and less than. For a couple years we did try having one set of kids open gifts on Christmas Eve (the others got to do a gift or two) with the other set waiting until Christmas Day. This did not really work either.

Our kids are older now, so as the holidays draw closer, we will be having a family discussion of what might work best over the two-day period, and what kind of outcomes we want to have. Maybe we do only stockings on the 24th and send some kids home with gifts to open Christmas Day. Or, maybe they will choose a large family gift that we can all share like a set of stand-up paddle boards or a mini vacation. Now that they are all older, maybe we can get together to open gifts Christmas night. I am not sure of the outcome yet, but I am willing to meet it with an open mind and heart.

Challenging Feelings to Consider
· ·

Again, the holidays are the hardest with feelings. I mentioned the gift giving inequity already, but there is still more to consider. As my girls got older, they had the choice to not go out of town to visit their dad over the holidays and they took it. Between friends, sports practice, jobs, and the desire to be with their stepsiblings they preferred to stay at home. This was devastating to their dad. I had them have a direct and kind conversation with him to share what was going on and had them choose alternate visit dates for the holidays. Allow your kids to speak on their own, you do not need to be the messenger. It is not perfect. I feel a bit guilty. But I hope it taught them how to have mature, hard conversations and to be prepared for the consequence (hurt feelings, compromise, etc.)

A last note. If there are specific holidays like Mother's Day or Father's Day, or a parent's birthday, please insist that your child spend time with that parent if possible. Allowing kids to have the choice to stay at home, or not show up for those specific days, creates divisive feelings in the family. They are missing a moment. Additionally, when the kids are younger, help them make cards or buy gifts for their other parent, your ex or theirs. That is their beloved parent and they want to be able to give them a surprise, not to mention it is a great feeling as a receiving parent. It is not about you. It is always about your kids.

LEAVE NOTHING UNCELEBRATED

I am a professional event planner and have been for over 25 years. Celebrating is in my DNA and "Leave Nothing Uncelebrated" is my life motto. This skill came in exceptionally handy when blending my family. For me, celebrating others is the greatest act of gratitude, love, and acknowledgment one can give to another. It allows you to recognize a person or a moment in time and create a vivid memory. This was my secret sauce in blending our bunch.

Early on, we created a "Feel Good Jar." This giant glass canister with lid lived on top of our fridge next to an assortment of gel pens and colorful patterned squares of paper. Our children were encouraged to write down a gratitude or a happy feeling and put it in the jar. They did not have to write their names, but we asked them to put a date on it (if they remembered). My husband and I also participated and even one of our babysitters! Eventually this practice tapered off as the kids got older and busier. But we have a collection of the sweetest, funniest notes written in their youthful scrawl. It gives an incredible glimpse into who they were at the time and what they valued. They wrote about themselves, their friends, school, their pets, and even their other families. It taught gratitude and helped give them the ability to stop and recognize a precious moment.

Family dinner time is always an opportunity to celebrate. We still go around the table and ask the kids to tell us the good news. Tell us about your day, what is on your mind, what are you working on? This allowed us to create a trusted space to share personal information and further recognize and celebrate them. It created gracious and patient listeners – my youngest daughter would tell us the minutiae of her day. "Well I was walking to the playground and I found a paperclip. Not just any paperclip, it was pink, and it was kind of buried underneath a pile of leaves. So, then I went and told my best friend, you know who that is right? I went to her pool party last year, and we kept digging through the leaves to see what else we could find..." on and on and on. You know I would give anything to have it back, and I will never get tired of hearing their stories.

Birthdays are a big deal, you were born! The "Birthday Fairy" shows up in the middle of the night to bring you into your new year with tons of decorations, balloons, a breakfast treat, and a small gift. Glitter is key. You get to pick the food you will eat that day including the birthday dessert, we leave love notes for you around the house, and we sing a special family birthday song. We do not always get to celebrate it on the exact day. Sometimes the kids do not wake up here and we do dinner instead. But we each go around the table and recognize something awesome about the birthday person and give them our wish for their year.

My husband has his own tradition that we all cherish. On our birthdays, Valentine's Day, or a large milestone (like graduation) he writes us personal letters. He picks out an appropriate and meaningful card which will hold a special letter, handwritten on his creamy ivory paper with his signature blue ink pen. It is the most precious gift. He is not outwardly emotional, but he is affectionate, and these letters are just another demonstration of his deep love and commitment to his family.

We celebrate every holiday we can think of, big or small. Chinese New Year: cultural food and music and reading of the different signs and history. Fat Tuesday: all the decadent food, music, King's Cake and history of the holiday. National Pancake Day, or Pizza Day, or French Fry Day – not so much history, but we serve it up with fun and decorations.

Lesson Learned
. . . .

We show up. Our kids show up. We celebrate each other and everything. We are our biggest fans. You will not get this time back.

Siblings will compare themselves to their brothers and sisters. They will feel less-than, better-than, or think the parents like one of them best, or that they do nothing right. This sucks, and as a parent you know how heart-breaking this can feel. Carve out one- on-one time with all your kiddos. Let them talk, you do the listening. Share with them what you like about them most, celebrate their accomplishments, and be generous with hugs and I love you.

This becomes especially important if there has been an argument, misunderstanding, or hurt feelings. After one particular moment of heated feelings with a stepdaugh-ter, I asked her to join me on a quick drive to the Sonic drive in to get everyone milkshakes. It gave us a moment to take a time out; listen to some music, calm down, and spend quality time together. It allowed me to ask her open-ended questions and assure her that even if we dis-agree, I will have her back.

Braden   12-31-12

When I went to
Coloraeo for cristmas
and thanks giving
that made me happy

VACATION, ALL I EVER WANTED

Another misnomer of the blended family is that you must do everything together. I learned firsthand this is not the case.

You will definitely need to schedule some blended family fun into your calendar. Travel options with five kids were extremely limited due to our budget and transportation options, so we have done many road trips. In fact, I think we've yet to fly somewhere all together. Day trips like hiking, biking, swimming, playing in the park, picnics, festivals, museums, the zoo are all great short options and start building new family memories.

Longer trips like camping or heading out of state take more coordination. Careful planning of baggage, food options, accommodations, and activities should be considered. For road trips, make sure each kid has a care package of snacks, toys, games, and their personal entertainment. Bring some car games, get a couple good books on tape, have a singing challenge, and prepare yourself to make several bathroom stops.

Blended family trips are fun, but trips with just one parent and their kids are equally important. It is a time to bond, make their own memories, and connect on a deeper family level. The kids need to feel a strong connection to their parent that has nothing to do with you. Put these very important dates on your calendar too. Help your spouse get organized and send them off with a big hug and words of encouragement. Take that time to recharge yourself or connect with your kids and family. You'll get to hear all about it soon enough.

Learn to give yourself and your spouse some private trips as well. It's important to stay connected to your spouse without your children, and it's important to recharge yourself as well. At the end of each July my kids attended a weeklong sleepaway camp. As a single mom, that is when I planned my personal travel or getaway. Once we blended a family, it seemed that we ended up getting the other set of kids for summer vacation that same week. I felt like I never got a break. I felt guilty that I wanted time to myself, resentful I was the main caregiver in our home, and insecure that I was less of a mom and more of an evil stepmom for wanting the time alone.

Give yourself and your spouse a break. Be honest with your feelings and be willing to compromise on the dates, the schedule, or activities that are planned during any breaks. Put your oxygen mask on first and take a few deep breaths. The bag may not inflate, but you'll be ready to better assist others.

Lesson Learned

. . . .

We have three kids with April birthdays, one with June, and one with December. The June and December kids always get screwed. Our June baby has had to travel on her birthday multiple years. Once for a family reunion, another time for a wedding; in general June is just a good time to travel and it is a great opportunity for a special experience.

One year on the road, we got her twelve presents for turning twelve. She was able to open one every hour on the hour while we were in the car. We spaced them out so that she could enjoy smaller trinkets, have a few fun things for the trip, and special big-ticket birthday items. When we stopped for the night, we gave her a couple choices for dinner and made sure to have some cake and sing. Make the effort to recognize the kid even during competing plans.

Challenging Feelings to Consider

. . . .

When you travel as a smaller bunch with just a singular parent and their kids, jealousy can rear its ugly head. The spouses may feel left out, and the kids may be envious of the trips the other kids get to take. This was true for us on multiple occasions. Three of our kids were competi-

tive gymnasts and got to travel all over the country (usually on planes) and participate in some fun sightseeing and adventures. When my youngest daughter (December baby) turned ten on the tenth, her magical birthday, I had worked for months to surprise her with a trip to Disney World and Harry Potter World with just her sister and grandparents. I even asked her dad to join us. It was an 'exclusive' small family trip and she almost never gets to have a birthday party with friends due to the holidays. But that still sucks for those left out.

All things can't be equal. One daughter got to go to Costa Rica with her Spanish class. One was active in DECA and went to California and Florida in one school year. Three of them were in a different state nearly every weekend for a few months and not always together. That is when you definitely need a tag team parent.

Keep a sense of adventure with your kids. Cherish the time you get to vacation with some or all of them. Choose a vacation or a spot that belongs to just your bunch and get to it as often as you can. Let the kids help you plan family outings and activities; remind them it's always about the time together.

When kids travel to see their bio parents out of state there are extra feelings to consider. Among them could be nervousness around navigating an airport, thinking they will get lost, or someone will forget to pick them up. They may be stressed about a change in routine, or they may be so crazy excited to hit the road, they will ask you incessantly *how much longer they have to wait until they get to go. That's a good thing.*

Even now when my daughters visit their dad, they often return melancholy and sad. My youngest will sometimes cry for a few days after and have trouble sleeping. This can also happen when kids arrive at the other parent's home. Children may experience homesickness and cry or act out for the other parent.

At first, I felt frustrated, but what I was truly lacking was empathy. For her, it's a fresh feeling of the loss of their parent all over again when she returns home. Remember, this is not about you. This is about your child's feelings tied to their relationship with the other parent, and a basic need of security. Be patient with yourself and them. Encourage them to reach out when they are sad or homesick during or following a visit. Give them space when they are spending time with the other parent. There's no need to text or call constantly, it's invasive to the child and the parent. Respect their time and relationship with the other parent. Give them a way to reach you at any time and let them decide when to do it. I promise they miss you too.

KEEP THE FAITH

Now more than ever, it is more common for blended families to have different views on religion. With several people of differing opinions in the mix it can feel overwhelming. My husband and I had different religious upbringings, but agreed on a specific set of values and faith that we wanted our family to follow. We prayed together as a family, but did not attend church services. Around middle school, each of our kids started to attend church in one form or another. They went with friends to youth groups, Young Life, Bible camp, or actual church services. A few of them decided to get baptized, which we supported. We valued their choices and were proud they chose independently. However, one of them became very vocal about their new beliefs and went a little too far, condemning the other siblings' choices or behavior with extreme viewpoints that we did not support. This became another opportunity for a conversation about beliefs, values, not standing in judgment, and being kind to others.

Lesson Learned

········ ··· ·······

Eventually we did go to church as a family. My husband's ex-wife and children found a church they liked, and we decided to join them. At first, it was wonderful. We loved sitting together as a family and would sometimes go out to eat afterwards. They had great music and inspirational messages, a strong community outreach, and a variety of family and youth programs. After attending for several months, the church had a call for volunteers. I filled out a form to work with high school-college ages (my sweet spot) and opened the intro email with excited anticipation. One of the requirements of volunteering was to formally join the church, which we had not done yet. As I reviewed the form, I noticed two beliefs that did not sit well with me. One, the church did not believe in living together before marriage, and we were not yet married. Two, their doctrine stated that being a homosexual was a sin against God, and by becoming a member you agreed to that belief. I do not agree with either of those views, at all. I requested a meeting with the youth pastors to ask my questions. Long story short — it was an incredibly disturbing meeting, and I was ineligible to volunteer due to living (in sin) with my partner outside of marriage, and believing that love is love, and LGBTQ people have equal rights. Devastated and crying I left the church and called my partner sobbing; not knowing that I was on speaker phone and a couple of the kids overheard what happened. Needless to say, my partner and I stopped attending immediately. We were open and honest with the kids re-

garding our experience and beliefs but did not insist that they make the same choice. Surprisingly – they were incredibly kind and supportive. While some of them continued to attend, they never treated me differently, and actually became less involved over time. Eventually they made the choice on their own to stop going based on their own experiences and beliefs.

Challenging Feelings to Consider

Your children are looking to you for guidance on your personal beliefs while they are actively asking questions and developing their own thoughts and opinions. Remember they are subject to a lot of outside influence with various family, friends, and social media. Keep the dialogue going. Be truthful. When we discuss something specific with religion, race, or politics I will often preface with "This is what I believe" or "This is what our family believes" and ask them what they think and feel. The number one rule in our family is to 'Be Kind.'

ARE WE THERE YET?

I am not sure what exact moment it was for our family, but I can tell you it took several years to feel really blended. There are so many amazing stops along the way. Hearing your entire group of kids laughing in the next room. Getting that unexpected hug or an "I love you" from a step-kid. Making it through a family event intact and with joy. Having an argument and coming back to a place of peace and forgiveness quickly. Knowing every kid's favorite food, color, style, music, book, game, preference, etc. and nailing it when it counts. Feeling a burning hot indignation when someone hurts one of any of your kid's feelings and you're ready to go mamma bear on the person that hurt your babies. Getting proudly introduced as a stepparent to their friends. Having one of your kids call you on the phone and ask for help. It is unique for every family.

One of mine just might have been the dinner conversation when our kids agreed they did not like to use the word "step" when describing their siblings. They prefer to say "my brother" or "my sister" without having to describe where exactly they are on the family tree because to them, it does not matter.

Finally getting married was a true celebration for all of us. The kids were old enough to participate and enjoy all of it. We kept it very small with just our kids and imme-diate family and made it a full weekend soiree. A couple interesting things happened in the process.

One night at dinner my youngest daughter asked my partner, "Why didn't you ask our permission to marry our mom?" He laughed and said "Well, we've been togeth-er for so long I didn't think I needed to." "Well you do!" she replied. Again, he stepped up to the plate and with sincerity said "I love all of you girls so much, and I have always considered you my family. Let's make it official. Can I marry your mom?" That was all she needed to hear.

The work of blending a family does not stop. To really be cohesive, include your kids in some decision making. We were not going to seek their marriage approval per se, but it was important for her to be on the journey with us. In-clusion is key to the blend.

Another evening as the wedding drew near, my daughter came into my bedroom. "Mom, I am really upset that you are changing your name. It feels like you won't belong to me anymore. You had the same last name (with the oldest) all through high school and now you won't with me." Wow. I never thought of that. I kept my first married last name for continuity with the girls in school and contemplated going back to my maiden name several times. I was excited to change my last name and 'belong' to my husband's family. I think I felt that act was MY official blending. The vulnerability she showed with me was a great opportunity to express my love and admiration to her and assure her even after all this time, nothing would break our bond. Especially not a last name.

family makes me
fell good wcn I
am sad I Love
my family I you you
from Taryn
December 31 2012

YOUR PERFECT BLEND

I want you to take a few minutes in a quiet comfortable space. Take some deep breaths and close your eyes. When you picture your blended family, what is your ideal vision? Is it an enjoyable meal? A happy holiday? Standing together at a wedding or graduation? Feeling like you are appreciated instead of hated? All your kids and grandkids surrounding you and your spouse at a milestone anniversary?

Your family belongs to you, with all of it's scabs, scars, stitches, and band aids. Embrace the cluster for what it is and keep your eyes on that goal.

It helped me to put up family and individual pictures and a few meaningful family-centric signs throughout our house. I created and brought to life the most vibrant image of a blended family my partner and I could imagine. That family was right in our face smiling at us and encouraging us not to give up. It really helped on the bad days.

I love you, and I admire what you are working towards. You

are important. You can do this.

Remember, 'Love Makes a Family' in all of it's messy, fabulous, fiery forms. Stay consistent, have compassion, be
humble, be honest, be kind. **And do not ever give up, even
on your hardest day.**

Life is hard. But I got this.
-Taitum
March 27, 2017

AUTHOR BIO

Tiffany Gravelle is an author, professional events planner, and business consultant, with over 25 years of experience in business development, leadership and managing high-performing teams - including her blended family of seven. She holds the Certified Meeting Planner (CMP) designation from the Events Industry Council and is a Credit Union Development Educator (CUDE).

When she is not celebrating everyone and everything by spreading joy and glitter, Tiffany is a mom of three teenagers and two adults, a mountain bike widow, lake rat, Red Sox fan, avid reader, foodie, and dog lover.

NOTES/RESOURCES

https://childrenssuccessfoundation.com/about-nurtured-heart-approach/more-about-the-nurtured-heart-approach/

https://www.urmc.rochester.edu/encyclopedia/content.aspx?ContentTypeID=1&ContentID=3051

https://psychcentral.com/lib/the-5-cs-of-effective-discipline-setting-rules-for-children/

CPSIA information can be obtained
at www.ICGtesting.com
Printed in the USA
BVHW031016201020
591410BV00003B/38

C000090062

GLASGOW

A Portrait | Roy Firth

Neil Wilson Publishing Ltd · Glasgow
www.nwp.co.uk

For Emlyn, Victoria, Joshua & Sefton

Neil Wilson Publishing Ltd
303 The Pentagon Centre
36 Washington Street
GLASGOW
G3 8AZ

Tel: 0141-221-1117
Fax: 0141-221-5363
E-mail: info@nwp.co.uk
http://www.nwp.co.uk

All illustrations and text
© Roy Firth, 2005

The author has asserted his
moral right under the
Design, Patents and
Copyright Act, 1988, to be
identified as the Author of
this Work. Reproduction of
all images is expressly
forbidden without the prior
consent of the Author and
Publisher.

A catalogue record for this
book is available from the
British Library.

ISBN 1-903238-79-X

Typeset in
Officina Sans Book

Designed by
Mark Blackadder

Printed and bound by
Oriental Press, Dubai

Frontispiece

The Doulton Fountain
Glasgow Green

First erected in Kelvingrove
Park for The Empire
Exhibition of 1888, the
fountain was a gift to the
city from Sir Henry
Doulton. Constructed of
terracotta, it was designed
by AE Pearce. In 1890 the
structure was moved to
Glasgow Green, but 100
years later the fountain
was suffering from neglect
and had dried up. Thanks
to a £4 million restoration,
it was moved piece by
piece in 2004 to its
present location in front of
The People's Palace. The
five tiers, containing
statues of inhabitants of
the Commonwealth
colonies, are topped by
Queen Victoria. At 14m
(46ft) high, this is the
world's largest terracotta
fountain.

Photograph opposite
title page

Glasgow coat-of-arms on
the Kelvin Bridge
Great Western Road

(see also page 70)

Contents

Broomhill Drive
West End

This is a typical
terrace of Victorian
four-storey, red,
sandstone tenements
which are often
beautifully lit by the
afternoon sun. Many
similar examples can
be found throughout
the city.

Scotland Street School
Scotland Street

This Charles Rennie Mackintosh
design of 1904 was fairly basic for a
school of that period. What was
exceptionally original, however, was
the detail — notably the two
curved, glazed stair towers above
the boys' and girls' entrances. (There
is even a separate entrance for the
infants). The 21 classrooms were
designed to accommodate 1250
pupils. The school is now Glasgow's
Museum of Education and as such is
open regularly to the public.

Firhill Stadium
Maryhill

Partick Thistle (aka The Jags or
The Maryhill Magyars) have been
playing at Firhill since 1909.
In 1922 they drew a crowd of
49,838 for a match against
Rangers. However, their finest
hour was in 1971 when they
defeated the all-conquering Celtic
4-0 in the League Cup Final.
Thistle are currently playing
outside the Premier League,
and Firhill's capacity, due to
modernisation is now 14,538.

My early memories of Glasgow go back to my
boyhood in the 1950's when I used to visit the
city from the family home in Ayrshire with my
father. We were mainly trainspotting or going to a
football match, but I remember the engine sheds
at Polmadie, Corkerhill and St Rollox which all held
a steamy fascination for me. And I remember
watching Ayr United win 3-0 at Ibrox!

Regrettably, during my studies at Strathclyde
University, I failed to appreciate Glasgow's architectural prowess. It was only after I joined the
Ordnance Survey and spent time in the city
revising Landranger maps that I took time to stop
and look around and above me. It was only then
that I realised what a wonderful city Glasgow was.
The stunning tenements of Broomhill (opposite)
and the work of Charles Rennie Mackintosh such as
Scotland Street School (opposite) took my breath
away. I was hooked.

My work with the Ordnance Survey took me all
over Britain, but for many years I was based in
Scotland, mapping the Highlands & Islands in
particular. During this time I started to take
photographs of landmarks and buildings and had
many pictures published on the covers of OS maps.

Following early retirement in 2004, I established a
home digital photographic laboratory and one of
my first thoughts was to take a closer look at
Glasgow's architectural heritage. I originally had a
working list of about 50 subjects, but following
further research, ground visits and consultation
with my publishers, the list just grew and grew.

My wish-list comprised public buildings, historic
sites, visitor attractions, monuments, churches,
bridges, significant architecture — indeed
anything that could be deemed a point of interest,
both ancient and modern. Of course there are
omissions and gaps — one book will never be
enough for Glasgow! I also included some world-
famous sites within an hour's drive of the city,
such as Burns Cottage and New Lanark. I hope the
images will encourage interest in some of the less
well known and less frequently visited sites in and
around Glasgow.

During my ground visits I became fascinated by
the way natural light can alter a building's
character. A seemingly dull façade by day can
come alive brilliantly when illuminated by the late
evening sunshine of mid-summer. If the book gives
the impression that the sun always shines on
Glasgow, I make no apologies for that.

My father is still with us, but alas! those smoky
engine sheds are no more, and the football
grounds have changed dramatically and much for
the better. Glasgow remains a wonderful, vibrant
city and I hope my book is a worthy of it.

Enjoy!

Roy Firth
June 2005

Auchentoshan Distillery
Dalmuir

This attractive whisky distillery, located close to the Erskine Bridge, was established in 1825. Its water source is Cochna Loch in the Kilpatrick Hills, and the name Auchentoshan is Gaelic for 'corner of the field'. Now owned by Morrison Bowmore Distillers, it continues to produce award-winning malts, involving a unique triple distillation process.

Bank of Scotland
St Vincent Street

Situated on the corner of Renfield Street and St Vincent Street, this building was constructed in 1924 to the designs of James Miller. He was inspired by a building on Broadway in New York. Giant Ionic columns embrace the lower three floors of what is the company's primary West of Scotland presence.

The Barras
Gallowgate

Accessed by arched entrances on London Road, Bain Street and Gallowgate, The Barras is Scotland's most famous market. At its liveliest on Sunday mornings, there are many outdoor stalls, however most traders operate within the old warehouses in the vicinity. A huge variety of items, both brand-new and second-hand are on offer e.g. clothes, furniture, jewellery and electronic goods.

Barrowland Ballroom
Gallowgate

The dance hall was opened in 1934, and is situated in the heart of The Barras market. For 40 years it was hugely popular with thousands of Glasgow dancers, despite a near disastrous fire in 1958. Bill Haley's only appearance in Scotland was at this venue in 1964. Today Barrowland, illuminated by distinctive neon lighting, is Glasgow's premier rock concert venue.

Bath Street
City Centre

Running from the city centre westwards to Charing Cross, Bath Street was opened in 1800 by the City Superintendent, James Cleland. The street was named after the Baths erected by William Harley, one of Glasgow's benefactors. Bath Street contains many fine two to four storey Georgian houses, which, although extensively altered within, still retain their outward splendour.

Broadcasting House
Queen Margaret Drive

Headquarters of the
BBC in Scotland, the
original building dates
back to 1869. It was
used as an art gallery
and a college before
being bought by the
BBC in 1935, since
when it has undergone
many renovations and
extensions in line
with the boom in
broadcasting.

Bells Bridge
Finnieston

This steel bridge was
constructed in 1988 for the
Glasgow Garden Festival
and now forms part of the
Clyde Walkway, linking the
Science Centre to the SECC.
Two of its three spans
pivot, allowing larger
boats, such as the *Waverley*,
to pass through.

Blythswood Square
Blythswood Hill

The square, one of Glasgow's finest, is bounded by West Regent Street, West George Street, Blythswood Street and Douglas Street. It was created in 1823 by William Garden and his architect John Brash, chiefly for the city's merchants. Retaining its early 19th-century design, it is now mainly occupied by offices.

14

Boclair House
Milngavie Road

This stunning red
sandstone building, with
its seven graceful arches in
its western elevation and
well maintained gardens, is
located near the centre of
Bearsden. Boclair House is
occupied by East
Dunbartonshire Council.

Botanic Gardens
Great Western Road

Botanic gardens have existed in Glasgow since 1705 at various sites. However the present one was established here in 1839 and now includes various laid out gardens, an arboretum, ornamental fountain, visitor centre and glasshouses. The most striking of these is the Kibble Palace, originally built at Coulport in 1865 and re-erected here in 1873. The main dome is 45m (146ft) in diameter and 13m (43ft) high. At the time of writing (2005) it is undergoing an extensive rebuild and is due to reopen in 2006.

Bothwell Castle
Uddingston

Situated ten miles east of the city centre and overlooking the Clyde, Bothwell is Scotland's largest and finest castle of the 13th century. The castle featured in many 14th-century sieges during the wars with England, and was home to the Black Douglases. Now in ruins, it is in the care of Historic Scotland.

Broomielaw
City Centre

During the 19th century the Broomielaw developed into one of the busiest and noisiest places in Glasgow, if not Scotland, with cargo ships berthing and trading here. Many warehouses sprang up, but as ship sizes increased, trade moved downstream. From Victorian times this was also the main embarkation point for trippers going 'doon the watter', particularly during the Glasgow Fair — the city's traditional holiday fortnight. Today little evidence of this activity remains, (certainly precious few boats), except the Clyde Navigation Trust Building, but there is some beauty in the graceful curves of stone, steel and glass.

Buchanan Street
City Centre

Commemorating merchant Andrew
Buchanan, this is probably
Glasgow's finest single street.
Until relatively recently it was one
of the city's main thoroughfares
connecting two mainline railway
stations — St Enoch and
Buchanan Street — both now
demolished. Pedestrianised in
1978, Buchanan Street contains
many high quality shops and
arcades.

Buchanan Galleries
Buchanan Street

This stone-clad shopping centre,
designed by Jenkins & Marr and
opened in 1998, is the largest city
centre development in Scotland. At
600,000 sq.ft. it is over twice the
size of the St Enoch Centre, and
contains over 80 quality shops.
Adjacent to mainline, underground
and bus stations, and close to the
M8 with 3000 car parking spaces,
it has proved highly successful.

Burns Cottage
Alloway

Lying 35 miles south of Glasgow, in the village of Alloway near Ayr, is Burns Cottage, birthplace of Robert Burns, Scotland's national bard. He was born here on January 25th 1759 — the simple clay and rubble cottage having been built by Burns' father two years earlier. Adjacent to the cottage is a museum containing many important Burns manuscripts and artefacts. The Cottage and museum, which are open throughout the year, form part of the Burns National Heritage Park and are now under the care of The National Trust for Scotland. An ambitious £10m revamp of the facility is planned to transform it into something approaching the massively successful development of William Wordsworth's home in Grasmere.

The Burrell Collection
Pollok Country Park

Situated within the heart
of Pollok Country Park, the
building was constructed
between 1972 & 1983 to
house the extraordinary
collection of artefacts
donated to the City by Sir
William Burrell (1861-
1958), a Glasgow shipping
magnate. The collection
of over 8000 pieces is
remarkable as it
encompasses examples
from many historic periods
and different continents.
Also displayed is a
reconstruction of one of
the rooms of Hutton
Castle, Sir William's home.
Externally the construction
is of pink sandstone,
stainless steel and glass.

Caledonia Road Church
Gorbals

Designed by Alexander
'Greek' Thomson, Glasgow's
most famous Victorian
architect, the church was
built in 1856. This was
Thomson's first church, and
preceded his other great
Glasgow work, St Vincent
Street Church. Although a
distinctive landmark, the
church is in fact a shell
following a fire in 1965,
and because of proposed
road developments, its
future is uncertain.

Castle Chambers
West Regent Street

On the junction of West
Regent Street and
Renfield Street, this fine,
baroque, red sandstone
block of eight storeys was
built for the MacLachlan
Brothers in 1902. The
brothers used the
building as headquarters
for their whisky business.
Castle Chambers is richly
adorned with carvings
and sculptures,
particularly around the
octagonal corner tower.

Cathkin Braes
Carmunnock

Cathkin Braes Country
Park lies about five
miles south of the city
centre, and from its
highest point of
192m(630ft), affords
panoramic views north-
wards over Glasgow and
towards the Campsie Fells
and the mountains of the
Southern Highlands. The
park covers nearly 500
acres and offers many
fine heathland and
woodland walks.

Celtic Park
Parkhead

Home to Celtic Football Club, the other half of the 'Old Firm', the club was formed in 1888 as a charitable trust to serve the poorer Catholic community of Glasgow's East End. The gates of Celtic Park opened on 20 August, 1892, and the ground developed into one of the largest in Britain — its record gate quoted as 92,000 (vs. Rangers on 1 January, 1938). In 1967, Celtic became the first British team to win the European Cup — remarkably with a team all hailing from Glasgow! Following the Taylor Report in 1990, Celtic made ground improvements and today the 60,000 all-seater Celtic Park is the second largest club ground in Britain.

Central Station
Gordon Street

Built by Blythe & Cunningham
between 1876 & 1879 for the
Caledonian Railway, Central Station
was extended in 1906 to
accommodate 13 platforms, making
it the city centre's most extensive
building. Today the station, which
is Scotland's busiest, is the
terminus of the electrified West
Coast main line from London, as
well as serving areas to the
south of the city, Greenock,
and the Ayrshire coast.

Central Thread Agency
Bothwell Street

Sitting between
Wellington Street and
West Campbell Street,
the former Central
Thread Agency was built
in three stages between
1891 and 1901 by H&D
Barclay. The upper four
floors are highly
decorated — the
eastern section being
the most lavish. The
building was the
headquarters of the
thread manufacturers
Coats Paton. Today a
large section of the
ground floor is occupied
by Marks & Spencer.

Chinatown
New City Road

Though smaller than other 'Chinatowns' in, for example, Manchester, Liverpool and London, Glasgow's version is nonetheless well worth a visit. The retail outlets are mainly housed in a warehouse-type building close to the M8, and the brick-built Gateway is typically adorned with lions and dragons.

Citizens Theatre
Gorbals

Opened in 1878 as Her Majesty's Theatre, the name was changed to Royal Princess' Theatre in 1880. The Citizens Company was founded in 1943, and in 1945 after WW2 it was re-opened as the Citizens Theatre. A fire in 1977 destroyed the original façade along with the neighbouring Palace Theatre. Today the Citizens, which offers a varied programme of productions, has three auditoria, the largest of which holds 600 people.

City Chambers
South Frederick Street

Built in 1883-89, this was an attempt by architect William Young to bring a little piece of Italy to Glasgow. Considered to be Glasgow's finest decorated building, it also enhanced its boast of being the Second City of The Empire. Its frontage dominates the eastern side of George Square, but however lavish the exterior may be, the interior either matches or surpasses it — particularly the marbled staircases and mosaics of the entrance hall. The City Chambers remain the seat of local government.

City Union Railway Bridge
City Centre

This bridge, opened in 1899 (William Melville, Engineer), was the first permanent Clyde bridge to have a steel superstructure. The bridge conveyed trains into the now demolished St Enoch Station, but since the 70s has carried a little used line over the Clyde. Of Gothic appearance, there are two castellated piers at each end.

Clyde Auditorium
Finnieston

Designed by Sir Norman Foster, this 1997 structure adjoins the SECC on the north side of the Clyde, and has quickly become one of Glasgow's most unique landmarks. The complex, distinctive shape has been likened to the Sydney Opera House, and has the obvious nickname of 'The Armadillo'. The auditorium is used for concerts and conferences and can seat 3000 people.

**Clyde Navigation
Trust Building**
Robertson Street

Constructed to J.J.
Burnet's designs over a 25-
year period from 1882 to
1907. The Trust, being one
of Glasgow's then most
important and wealthy
bodies, demanded a
building to rival that of
the City Chambers.
Externally the most
striking feature is the
impressive dome (on the
corner of The Broomielaw)
rising above statues of
Europa and Amphitrite.
Internally the building is
no less lavish, but with
the decline in shipping
over the last century, it is
now occupied by the less
powerful Clydeport.

Co-operative Buildings
Morrison Street

This wondrous, massive, neo-classical building was constructed in 1897 by Bruce & Hay for the Scottish Co-operative Wholesale Society. Designed as a warehouse to eclipse all others in scale and elaboration, it now sits adjacent to the southern approach of the Kingston Bridge.

CO·OPERATIVE WHOLESALE

County Buildings and Courthouses
Wilson Street

Built in 1844 by Clarke
& Bell to replace The
Tolbooth, this Greek
Revival building was
itself made redundant
when the Council moved
to the City Chambers in
1888. Pictured here is
the massive south
portico of six Ionic
columns sitting above a
plinth carved with
classical figures. Today
there is an ongoing
conversion scheme.

Crookston Castle
Brockburn Road

The castle lies five miles south of the city centre in Pollok. Although there has been a castle on this prominent hill from the 12th century, this present structure dates from around 1400, and was long the property of the Stuarts of Darnley. Of the original four towers, only one remains. Now in the care of Historic Scotland, the castle is open to visitors, and a fine view of Glasgow is achieved by climbing the stairs to the top of the tower.

Dolores Ibárruri
(La Pasionaria)
Clyde Street

This statue, on the
north bank of the
Clyde, not far from
Glasgow Bridge,
commemorates the
65 Glasgow
volunteers who died
in the Spanish Civil
War (1936-39).
Dolores Ibárruri
(1895-1989) was a
communist politician
who fought against
Franco.

Dumbarton Castle
Dumbarton

Twelve miles from
Glasgow and set in
the 76m (250ft)
Dumbarton Rock, the
castle is one of the
oldest fortified sites
in Britain. (The name
Dumbarton comes
from 'Dun Breatann'
— fortress of the
Britons). A stronghold
can be traced here
back to the 5th
century. Today
Dumbarton Castle is
in the care of Historic
Scotland and is open
all year round.

**Easterhouse
Phoenix**
Easterhouse Road

This sculpture was
created in 2000 by
local artist Andy
Scott, who was
also responsible
for the Heavy
Horse on the M8.
*The Phoenix rising
from the Ashes* is
a community
initiative, and
represents the
regeneration of
the surrounding
area.

Egyptian Halls
Union Street

Located opposite Central Station's Union Street entrance and built in 1871-73 to Alexander Thomson's design, the façades of the four cast-iron floors are all different. However, the building takes its name from the 19 squat Egyptian-detailed columns along the top floor. Now sadly neglected.

Finnieston Crane
Finnieston

A massive landmark and
symbol of the city
standing on the north
bank of the Clyde adjacent
to the SECC. Constructed
by Cowans Sheldon in
1932, the 59m (195ft)
crane could lift locomo-
tives and military tanks,
weighing up to 178
tonnes, into cargo ships.
Now preserved in working
order as an industrial
monument, the crane is
also illuminated at night.

Fish Market
Clyde Street

Built in 1873 by Clarke & Bell
and encompassing the
handsome Merchants Steeple,
the building ceased to be a
market in 1977. Known locally
as The Briggait, the fine
galleried hall was restored in
1986. Externally the eleva-
tions are French Renaissance,
the cast-iron gates surrounded
by coats-of-arms, fish, Queen
Victoria and hippocampuses
(sea-monsters).

Gallery of Modern Art
Royal Exchange Square

Originally built as a private
residence for tobacco merchant
William Cunninghame in 1780,
the 12-pillared Corinthian
portico, clock tower and hall
were added later. The hall itself
has been used to trade in
tobacco, sugar, rum, coal, iron
and shipping. Baron Marochetti's
statue of the mounted
Wellington was completed in
1844. Since 1996 it has been
used to display the city's
collection of contemporary
work by local, national and
international artists.

George Square
City Centre

The square was first laid out in 1785, with three-storey houses surrounding private garden areas. However, during Victorian times, the square grew in importance with the arrival of the City Chambers. Today the Copthorne Hotel on the north side is the only evidence of the original Georgian scheme. Queen St Station and the (former) Head Post Office have also been built around the edge. Sir Walter Scott sits atop of the tall column in the centre, with 10 other statues of Glasgow worthies including Robert Burns scattered around the square. Conspicuous by his absence is George III after whom the square is named. The square is a focus of ceremonial, symbolic and political Glasgow.

Glasgow Bridge
City Centre

Also known as the Jamaica Bridge, this is the third bridge built on this site (1895-99, Blyth & Westland). The original plans for this bridge bore no resemblance to an earlier bridge by Thomas Telford. However, following a public outcry, the plans were altered to resemble Telford's structure — having seven arches and using much of the old bridge's stonework.

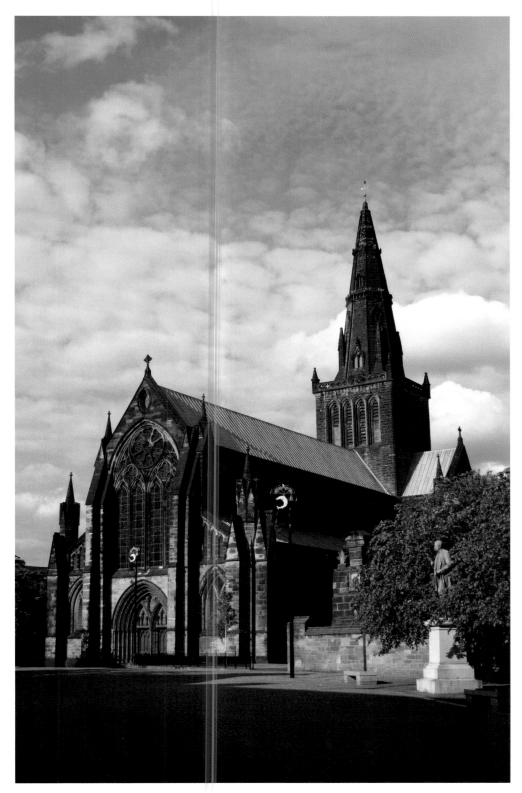

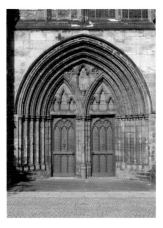

Glasgow Cathedral
Cathedral Square

Also known as the Cathedral of St Mungo (Glasgow's patron saint), the present Gothic building was started in the 13th century and completed in the 15th century. It is the only medieval cathedral on the Scottish mainland to have survived the 1560 Reformation relatively intact. Set deep into the Molindinar Burn hillside, the Cathedral houses a double choir, one on top of the other. Further attractions include a vaulted crypt, a 15th-century stone screen, carved stones and the Blackadder Aisle. Historic Scotland manage the Cathedral.

Glasgow Central Mosque
Gorbals

A landmark on the south bank of the Clyde with its golden dome, the mosque was built in 1984 and has become the focal centre of Glasgow's Muslim community. Although it was not until 1916 that the first Indian immigrant arrived in Glasgow, many thousands arrived throughout the rest of the 20th century, the numbers increasing due to problems following the partitioning of India and Pakistan in 1947. Many of the largely Pakistani Muslims settled in areas on the south side of the city, such as Pollokshields and the Gorbals, hence the situation of this mosque.

Glasgow Savings Bank
Ingram Street

This building, formerly the
Glasgow Savings Bank (1894-
1900, J.J. Burnet) sits on the
corner of Ingram Street and
Glassford Street, and the
immediate architectural
landscape has remained
virtually unchanged since
Victorian times. This building,
which has Glasgow's Coat of
Arms and a statue of St
Mungo above the main
entrance, also has a
magnificent glazed dome.
Today this building now
houses a clothing shop.

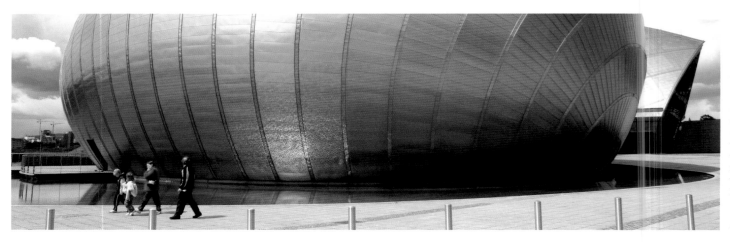

Glasgow Science Centre
Pacific Quay

Opened by Queen Elizabeth II in July 2001, the Glasgow Science Centre is the result of a Millennium Commission Lottery funded project, and occupies the site of the 1988 Garden Festival. The centre comprises three main attractions; a multi-storey, titanium-clad, interactive Science Mall (including a theatre), Scotland's first IMAX cinema, and a 105m-high fully rotating tower (Scotland's tallest building) complete with viewing platform. The centre is linked by two bridges; the Millennium Bridge and the Bells Bridge, over the Clyde, to the SECC and Clyde Auditorium.

Glasgow Necropolis
Cathedral Precinct

Occupying a hill to the east of Glasgow Cathedral, the Necropolis was laid out in 1833 to the design of John Bryce, and was inspired by the Pere Lachaise cemetery in Paris. Best approached from John Knox Street, over the Bridge of Sighs, there is a maze of roads and paths running past a fascinating collection of Victorian tombs and memorials. The most prominent of these is that of John Knox, which in fact dates back to 1825. Seldom used for burials today, the Necropolis is open to the public.

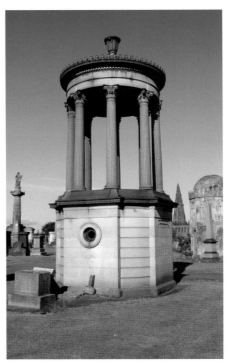

Glasgow School of Art
Renfrew Street

Regarded as Charles
Rennie Mackintosh's (and
indeed Glasgow's!) archi-
tectural masterpiece, the
building was constructed
in two phases from 1879
to 1909 following a
competition won by
Honeyman & Keppie —
CRM being their chief
designer. Combining
elements from traditional
Scottish architecture and
the Modern Movement,
the Renfrew Street façade
contains the studio
windows and the main
entrance, — sandstone,
glass and wrought
ironwork combining
together beautifully.
Also of note are the
magnificent three-storey
high library windows in
Scott Street. Glasgow
School of Art graduates
continue to be highly
regarded throughout
the world.

Glengoyne Distillery
Dumgoyne

This distillery was established in 1833. Sitting below the very prominent hillock of Dumgoyne (427m) at the western edge of the Campsie Fells on the A81, the distillery is 24km (15 miles) north of Glasgow. The name comes from Glen Guin (Glen of the Wild Goose). Regarded as the most southerly of the Highland malts, it is currently owned by Ian Macleod Distillers Ltd. The distillery is open all year round for visits and tours.

Govan Town Hall
Govan Road

Designed by Thomson and Sandilands, this building was opened in 1901. It is Glasgow's finest Beaux Arts Building, with its grand Greek portico over the main entrance, topped by an impressive dome. The design celebrates Govan's shipbuilding prowess of the time, and is adorned by several busts of local government officials. Inside there is a fine floor mosaic of the Govan Burgh Coat of Arms. The building remains in use today.

Graham Square
Gallowgate

This 1999 devel-
opment by Molendinar
Park Housing
Association, has
retained the original
elevation of the
former sand-stone
meat market. The free
standing B-Listed
wall is pinned back
using a special
support system,
creating a very
unusual visual effect.

Great Western Road
Kelvinbridge

Running from the
city centre along the
A82, this is the
traditional route
towards Dumbarton,
Loch Lomond and
the Western
Highlands. This
classic view is
looking westwards
towards Kelvinbridge.

Great Eastern Hotel
Duke Street

Designed by Charles Wilson as a cotton
spinning mill for Alexander's, the thread
manufacturers, this building opened in
the 1840s. Its classical bulk conceals a
cast-iron fireproof frame. In 1907, the
mill was converted into a hotel for
homeless men, providing accommodation
for 450. However, in August 2001 the
Great Eastern shut its doors for the last
time, opening again briefly in October
of that year for a public exhibition of
photographs displaying images of
'hotel life'. Current plans are to
convert this building into flats.

53

Greenbank
Clarkston

Six miles south of Glasgow lies the National Trust for Scotland property of Greenbank. The walled gardens in the grounds of Greenbank House contain some 3600 plant specimens, and are open to the general public all year round. The actual house is only open from Easter to October. The house and the land were gifted to the Trust in 1976 by Mr and Mrs William Blyth.

Hampden Park
Mount Florida

Completed and opened in 1903 to the designs of the renowned Archibald Leitch, Hampden was, and still is, home to Queens Park — an amateur side playing in the senior professional leagues. By 1937, Hampden's capacity had been increased to 150,000, making it then the world's largest stadium. It hosted virtually all of Scotland's Home International fixtures and domestic cup finals, and still does. The ground broke all attendance records — the highest being the 150,239 plus that turned out for the Scotland vs England match in 1937. Between 1981 and 1998, £63M was spent on the ground, turning it into a modern 52,000 all-seater stadium, which was reopened in 1999. The stadium is also home to the Scottish Football Museum.

The Hatrack
St Vincent Street

A superb building
in the Glasgow style
(1902, James Salmon
II). Ten visually
different floors
within one house
plot, all heavily
adorned with
cornicing, mouldings
and sculptures —
but predominantly
glass! The name
'Hatrack' was
derived from the
now missing peaked
roofscape.

The Heavy Horse
Easterhouse

Situated at Junction 9 off the M8 motorway, this magnificent 4.5m steel Clydesdale horse has become one of the city's most prominent landmarks. Unveiled in 1997, the sculptor was Andy Scott.

Hielanman's Umbrella
Argyle Street

An extension of the
Central Station viaduct
(1901-06, James
Miller), this was the
traditional meeting
place of highland folk
in Glasgow. Now,
beautifully restored,
of particular note are
the iron pillars and
tall classical windows.

High Court of Judiciary
Saltmarket

Adjacent to the Albert
Bridge and opposite the
entrance to Glasgow
Green, the court was
completed in 1811 by
William Stark. Its
Saltmarket façade has
Glasgow's earliest Greek
Doric portico. The court
was extended in 1997 and
the entire building is now
Glasgow's High Court.

The Hill House
Helensburgh

Helensburgh lies 22 miles west of Glasgow on the north bank of the Firth of Clyde. It was here in 1902 that the publisher Walter Blackie commissioned Charles Rennie Mackintosh to design not only a house and gardens, but the interior and furnishings also. The result was the Hill House, which remains CRM's finest domestic design. Donated to The National Trust for Scotland in 1982 by the Hill House Trustees, the house and gardens are open from Easter to October.

Horse Shoe Bar
Drury Street

Opened in 1872, this bar
has become one of the
City Centre's most famous
hostelries. The horseshoe
shaped bar was, for a
long time, the longest in
Britain at over 30m
(100ft). It is said that if
you stay in the Horse
Shoe Bar long enough,
you will meet everyone
that you have ever
known in your life!

House for an Art Lover
Bellahouston Park

This Art Nouveau building is the result of plans drawn up by Charles Rennie Mackintosh for a competition in a German magazine in 1901. Built on the site of Ibrox Hill House in 1989-96, it was a joint venture between Glasgow City Council, Graham Roxburgh and Professor Andy Macmillan, the architect. The key rooms in the house, which is rectangular in plan, are; the Dining Room, the Music Room and the Oval Room. The exterior is adorned with Art Nouveau relief sculptures. Both house and gardens are open to the public.

Hunterian Museum
University of Glasgow
The oldest public museum in Scotland was opened in 1807, in the University of Glasgow, which was then sited on High Street. In 1870, when the University moved to its present site — west of the city, the museum was re-housed within Sir George Gilbert Scott's fine neo-Gothic building. The collection founded by Sir William Hunter (1718-83), a former student, includes; books, coins, medals, paintings, rocks, minerals and medical & zoological specimens.

Hunterian Art Gallery
University of Glasgow

Founded by Dr. William Hunter in 1807, this is an outstanding collection of European art, including works by Rembrandt, Pissarro and Rodin. There are also major exhibits by the Scottish Colourists, and a graphics collection of some 30,000 prints. The building, which is open to the public, has a pleasant light and airy interior, and is located next to the University Library.

Hutchesons' Hall
Ingram Street

This building, erected between 1802-05 (David Hamilton), boasts a magnificent clocktower which is a famous landmark of Glasgow. It was originally commissioned and funded by the Hutcheson Brothers, philanthropists who previously supported a hospital for elderly men. The main body of the building is flanked by two statues of the brothers (brought from the hospital). These are the only 17th century statues remaining in Glasgow. Redeveloped by John Baird II in 1876, Hutchesons' Hall is now owned and used as offices and a shop by the National Trust for Scotland.

Ibrox Stadium
Edmiston Drive

Home to Rangers Football Club, founded in 1873, and one half of the famous 'Old Firm'. Ibrox was opened on 30 December 1899, and the magnificent main stand, designed Archibald Leitch was added in 1929. In January 1939 Ibrox packed in 118,567 (vs. Celtic — of course!), a record for any league match in Britain. However, following the disaster of 2 January 1971, when 66 people were killed, the appearance of the Stadium changed dramatically. Three, almost identical stands, now surround the heightened Leitch main stand, giving Ibrox an all-seated capacity of 50,411.

Italian Centre
Ingram Street

Situated in Glasgow's Merchant
City, this redevelopment
(1987-89, Page and Park),
includes a building that was
formally the Bank of Scotland.
The rooftop is adorned with
various Italian statues, and the
internal courtyard contains
interesting artefacts. The
Italian Centre is very popular,
housing several Italian
designer shops and pavement
cafés situated around an
impressive statue of Mercury.

John Street Arches
John Street

These triumphal arches (1913-23, Watson, Salmond & Gray), link the City Chambers main building to the eastern extension. The centre-piece of both sets of arches displays the Glasgow Coat of Arms, alongside various other intricate carvings.

Kelvin Bridge
Great Western Road

Kelvin Bridge (1889-91,
R Bell & D Miller), also
known as Great Western
Bridge is the 3rd bridge
in the vicinity spanning
the River Kelvin. The
striking cast iron bridge
is painted in stunning
green, has Gothic style
balustrades and displays
various badges
including the Glasgow
Coat of Arms. The
bridge was officially
opened on 29
September 1891.

**Kelvingrove Art Gallery
and Museum**
Argyle Street

This splendid building by J.W.
Simpson & Milner Allen was opened
in 1902 and sits in the beautiful
surroundings of Kelvingrove Park. In
red Renaissance, the galleries extend
from the high-roofed main hall, its
twin towers facing the University. It
houses one of the greatest civic
collections in Europe, including
armoury, natural history, Egyptian
and prehistoric artefacts, in addition
to significant collections of Dutch
and Italian Painting. Currently
closed for refurbishment, it will
re-open in 2006.

Completed in 1896
and designed by
Alexander Skirving —
a pupil of 'Greek'
Thomson. This
impressive Graeco-
Roman building was
originally known as
Langside Free Church,
and was Glasgow's
last classical church.
It is now used as a
bar/restaurant.

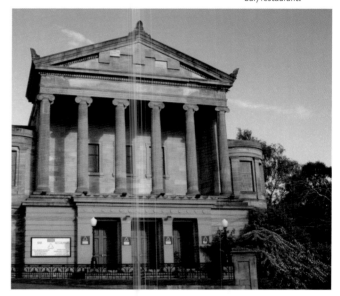

King's Theatre
Bath Street

This grand red sandstone
building (1901-04, Frank
Matcham), is situated on the
corner of Bath Street and
Elmbank Street. Originally
one of Britain's top rated
theatres, it was designed to
accommodate audiences of
2000. The exterior of the
building has various shaped
windows and stone
balustrades. Internally, it
has a lavish marbled foyer
and a magnificent domed
auditorium. Recently
refurbished, the King's Theatre
remains widely acclaimed
for its extravagant
pantomime productions.

This highly decorated 18m (58ft) pillar (1887-88, Alexander Skirving) commemorates the Battle of Langside, which took place on 13 May 1568 in this vicinity. The battle was fought between the forces of Mary Queen of Scots and those of the Regent Moray. This was the Queen's final defeat in Scotland. The monument, which sits in the middle of a roundabout, is topped by a lion resting his paw on a cannonball.

Liberal Club
Nelson Mandela Place

Standing at the junction
with Buchanan Street, this
fine red Dumfriesshire
sandstone building was
originally designed as the
Liberal Club in 1909 by A.N.
Paterson. At the entrance
there are two carved lions
and initials GLC (Glasgow
Liberal Club). The building
was used by the Scottish
Academy of Music and Drama
from 1928-80. Currently the
building is up for sale.

The Lighthouse
Mitchell Lane

Formerly *The Glasgow Herald* Building, by Charles Rennie Mackintosh (1893-95), The Lighthouse is a result of a £13 million conversion which was opened by HM Queen Elizabeth II in July 1999. The building is now home to Scotland's Centre for Architecture and Design. Covering six floors, The Lighthouse, which is open to the public, offers a changing programme of displays and exhibitions. A walk up the spiral staircase to the top of the Mackintosh Tower is rewarded with splendid views of the City Centre.

This magnificent bronze statue depicts an actual incident when David Livingstone, the missionary and explorer, was attacked by a lion. The animal was chased away, but not before Livingstone's arm was broken in two places. The sculpture sits beside The David Livingstone Centre in Blantyre and was commissioned by Ray Harryhausen, husband of Livingstone's great-grand-daughter, and modelled by Gareth Knowles in 2004.

Lobey Dosser Statue
Woodlands Road

This statue (1992, Tony Morrow and Nick Gillon), was created to commemorate the creator of the Lobey Dosser cartoon (Bud Neill 1911-70). The much loved cartoon initially appeared in the Glasgow *Evening Times* in 1949, and quickly gained a cult following. The statue is allegedly the only two legged equestrian statue in existence!

Mackintosh House
University of Glasgow

This building, although not spectacular from the outside (or indeed accessible!), contains an exceptional reconstruction of the home at 78 Southpark Street (now demolished) that Charles Rennie Mackintosh and his wife Margaret Macdonald lived in between 1906-14. All aspects of the house from the lighting, room sizes, interior décor, door frames, colour schemes, furniture and of course design have been beautifully recreated to the exact specification of the original house. Using the furniture from Mackintosh's marital home, the overall effect and detail of this house is spectacular.
This house can only be accessed via the Hunterian Art Gallery.

Mains Castle
East Kilbride

This 15th-century
tower house sits on
the edge of East
Kilbride and
overlooks the James
Hamilton Heritage
Park lake. Originally
the property of the
Comyns, the estate
was passed to the
Lindsays of Dunrod.
Now privately owned,
the castle's five
floors have been
recently restored.

Martyrs' Public School
Parson Street

Built in 1895-98 by
Charles Rennie Mackintosh
on the street where he
was born! This solid
three-storey sandstone,
former school, is topped
by three distinctive
ventilators, and still
survives despite extensive
adjacent road improve-
ments at the top of High
Street. Now
jointly used by a
theatre company and
Glasgow Museums.

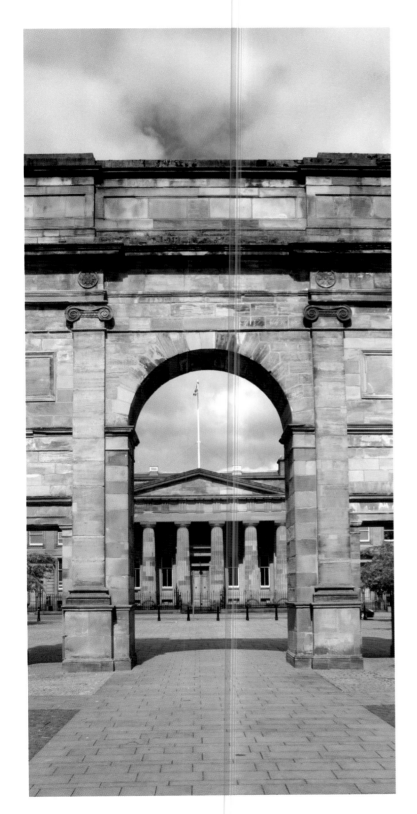

McLennan Arch
Glasgow Green

This grand structure now forms the Saltmarket entrance to Glasgow Green. Designed in 1792 by Robert and James Adam, the arch originally formed the centre-piece of Robert Adam's Assembly Rooms in Ingram Street, and was bequeathed by Bailie James McLennan MP to his fellow citizens. These rooms were demolished in 1890, and the arch was moved to three different locations, before finally arriving in its current position in 1990.

Mercat Cross
Glasgow Cross

This cross was designed by Edith Burnet Hughes and was inaugurated in 1930. It replaces the one that was removed from Glasgow Cross in 1659. Monuments such as these traditionally mark the spot where markets took place. This modern octagonal structure is topped by a shield-bearing unicorn. On its base can be found the city's Coat of Arms with its motto — 'Let Glasgow Flourish'.

Merchants' House Buildings
West George Street

On the corner of Queen Street, opposite the station, this structure faces George Square. Designed by John Burnet and completed in 1874, an additional two storeys were added in 1909. The building is crowned with a domed tower complete with a globe and a ship, symbolising Glasgow's world-wide trade at that time.

82

Mitchell Library
North Street

This is one of Glasgow's finest Edwardian, baroque buildings (1906-11, W.B. White), and is spectacular when floodlit at night. It was extended between 1972-80, and the rear of the building, in Granville Street, contains a 60m (200ft) long classical façade in three sections with a grand entrance adorned by 16 Ionic columns and various stone statues. (This was previously St Andrews Halls by James Sellars, 1874-77). Opened in 1911, the front façade is flanked by columns and balustrades and crowned with a magnificent green dome. Internally, the library is lavishly decorated, complete with marble staircase. Containing over one million pieces of literature, the Mitchell Library is one of the largest public reference libraries in Europe.

Montrose Street
Merchant City

23 Montrose Street
(1894, A.B.
MacDonald) occupies
the corner of Cochrane
Street, behind the City
Chambers extension.
With its pedimented
corner tower, Venetian
windows and baroque
detail, its style has
been described as
'unfriendly Victorian'.
Now disused, it was
last occupied by the
Department of
Environmental Health.

Nelson Mandela Place
City Centre

This square, situated at the intersection of Buchanan Street and West George Street was renamed Nelson Mandela Place (previously St George's Place) in 1986, to honour his anti-apartheid political stance in South Africa. This particular square was chosen because the South African Consulate was located here at the time. In the centre of the square stands St George's Tron Parish Church.

Nelson Monument
Glasgow Green

Built in 1806 and designed by David Hamilton, this was Britain's first monument to Viscount Horatio Nelson who had died a year earlier in 1805. At the base are engraved the names of his victories, including Trafalgar where he was killed. The monument is 44m (144 ft) high, and was damaged by lightning in 1810.

New Lanark
Lanark

A World Heritage
Site, the village of
New Lanark was
constructed over 200
years ago, when
David Dale built a
series of mills beside
the Clyde. The mills'
manager, Robert
Owen, provided
quality housing for
his work force, in
addition to schools
and the world's first
co-operative food
store. Today the
mills and the village
are stunningly
restored, attracting
some 400,000
visitors each year.

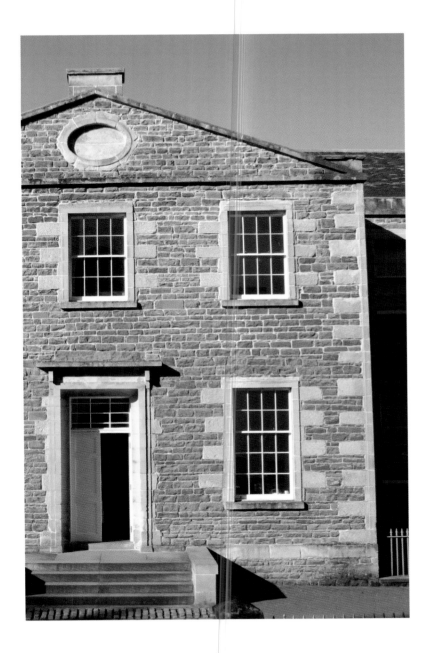

Newark Castle
Port Glasgow

Newark Castle is an attractive 3 storey tower house on the south bank of the Clyde. It dates from the 15th century and for many years was in the ownership of the Maxwells. However, in 1694 the castle was sold and leased to tenants. There is a fine doocot in the grounds, but also in close proximity to the west is a shipyard. Newark Castle is now in the care of Historic Scotland.

Òran Mór
Byres Road

Formerly the Old Kelvinside Parish Church, and sympathetically converted at a cost of £6m, this landmark is now a regular arts, music and culture venue at the top of Byres Road adjoining Great Western Road.

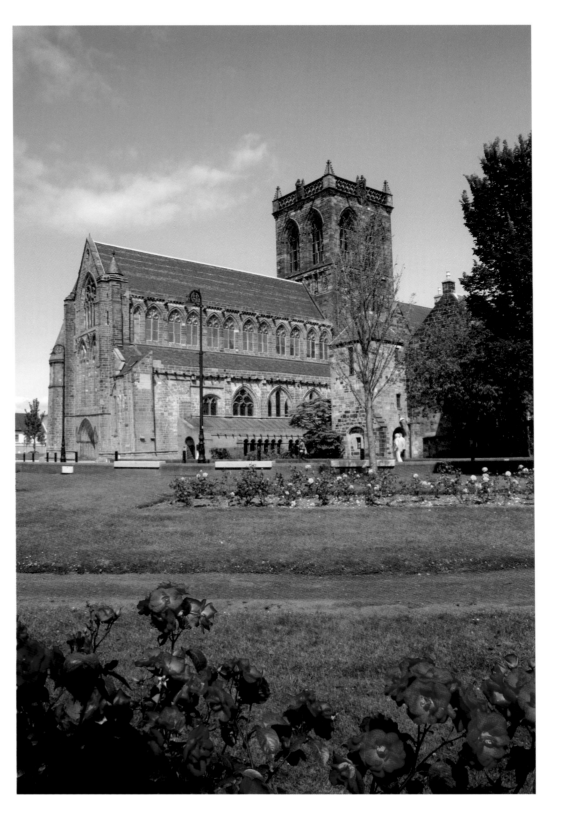

Paisley Abbey
Paisley

This wonderful building in the heart of Paisley dates from the 13th century, although a monastery was founded here by a community of Cluniac monks in 1163. Amongst the treasures within the Abbey are the 10th century Barochan Cross and an important collection of stained glass in the 14th-century nave. Visitors are welcome, and the Abbey has an exhibition of its history, a shop and café.

Park Church
Lynedoch Place

All that remains of the Victorian style, Park Parish Church (1856-58, John Thomas Rochead), is the tall, elegant, white painted tower. The church itself was demolished in 1968, and replaced by office buildings that are not in keeping with their Victorian surroundings.

Pavilion Theatre
Renfield Street

This imposing
building (1902-04,
Bertie Crew) is French
Renaissance in
design. The façade is
adorned with various
theatrical subjects.
Internally, the theatre
is lavishly decorated
in Louis XV style, and
has a seating
capacity of 1,800.
Charlie Chaplin is one
of the many famous
artists who performed
in this theatre
(previously known
as The Palace of
Variety).

People's Palace
Glasgow Green

Completed in 1984 by A.B.
MacDonald, the People's
Palace was designed for
everyone.
The building is red sandstone
in the French Renaissance
style, and contains the
people's history of Glasgow —
reconstructions of tenements
and single ends, and a wealth
of other recent Glasgow
memorabilia are on display.
At the rear of the building are
the fabulous Winter Gardens,
a huge glass conservatory
housing many exotic plants
and a coffee house.

Provand's Lordship
Castle Street

Glasgow's oldest house was built by Bishop Muirhead in 1471 as part of St Nicholas' Hospital. It faces the Cathedral and the more recent St Mungo Museum. Over the years, its many uses include being a manse, an alehouse, a sweetshop and accommodation for the local hangman! Quite plain on the outside, the main building has three floors each with three rooms. A museum since 1970, visitors also have the opportunity to enjoy the St Nicholas Gardens laid out in 1985.

The Piping Centre
Cowcaddens Road

At the top of Hope Street, Glasgow's Piping Centre was formally the Cowcaddens Free Church of Scotland (1872-73, Campbell Douglas & Sellars). The structure has an Italianate tower and a Greek-style portico. The centre is primarily used as a museum, exhibiting various bagpipes, some of which date back to Roman times.

Pollok House
Pollok Country Park

Designed by William Adam and completed by his son John in 1752, this Palladian mansion, with attached stables and walled garden, sits beside the White Cart Water. For many years it was occupied by the Maxwells, but in 1966 they donated the house to the City of Glasgow. It is now managed by the National Trust for Scotland and visitors are able to view fine collections of antique furniture, ceramics and paintings in addition to the servants' quarters.

Princes Square
Buchanan Street

Occupying the Prince of
Wales Buildings (1854,
John Baird), the
courtyard has been
given a huge glass
roof, covering 4 floors
of specialist and
designer shops. Inside,
escalators and ornate
stairways give access
to the shops and cafés.
Also of note is the
curious Foucault
pendulum. The square
was officially opened
by HRH Prince of Wales
on 29 April 1988.

Provan Hall
Garthamlock

This interesting, but little known, 15th-century building sits in what is now Auchinlea Park overlooking a small loch. It was built as a country retreat for a Glasgow Cathedral canon, Pebendary of Lanark — his townhouse being what is now Provand's Lordship. The small house has an attractive courtyard with an arched gateway, and a stone flight of stairs leading to the first floor. Although owned by the National Trust for Scotland, it is still in the council's care and open to the public.

PS Waverley
Lancefield Quay

Clyde-built in 1947, this vessel replaced the original *Waverley* which was sunk at Dunkirk in 1940. The 693-ton ship originally carried 900 passengers, and plied her trade on the Clyde before being sold for £1 in 1974 to The Paddle Steamer Preservation Trust. Following various refits she now tours the waters and ports of the UK in the summer, but returns to her new berth in Glasgow during winter. The *Waverley* is the last sea-going paddle-steamer in the world.

Queen Street Station
City Centre

The station was opened in 1842 following the construction of a 1 km ($^2/_3$ mile) tunnel from Cowlairs, bringing the lines of the Edinburgh and Glasgow Railway Company into the city. The magnificent vaulted roof, the last remaining in Scotland, spanning 76m (250ft) and 24m (78ft) high, was designed by James Carswell, commencing in 1878. Today Queen Street is the starting point for services to Edinburgh, Dundee, Inverness and Aberdeen, and the West Highland lines to Oban and Fort William.

Queen's Cross Church
Garscube Road

Also known as the
Mackintosh Church
(1879), this was
Charles Rennie
Mackintosh's only
church design to be
actually built. Its
distinctive red
sandstone tower is
close to Firhill
Stadium. Highlights
of the interior are the
stained glass and
wood and stonework
relief carving. The
building is the
international HQ of
the CRM Society.

Queen's Park
Queen's Park

This public park, on the south side of the city, covering 60 hectares (148 acres), is named after the area within which it is located — Queen's Park, which in turn was named after Mary, Queen of Scots. Opened in 1862, it was laid out by Joseph Paxton, the famous Victorian landscape gardener. The main entrance, the Art Nouveau park gates, is in Queen's Drive facing Victoria Road. Amongst the Park's attractions is the Glass House with its exotic plants and reptile house.

Ramshorn Kirk
Ingram Street

Riverside House
Clyde Street

Alternatively known as
St David's, Ramshorn
was designed by Thomas
Rickman and completed
in 1826. Gothic in style,
the church contains
impressive stained glass
windows. The tower is
quite a landmark in the
Merchant City and has
now been converted into
the Ramshorn Theatre of
Strathclyde University.

This simple red
sandstone building
stands at the northern
end of Portland Street
Suspension Bridge,
overlooking the Clyde.
Designed as a
warehouse by Eric
Sutherland, and built
in 1907, its seven
floors are topped by
two distinctive
pointed turrets.

**Robert Pollok
Memorial**
Eaglesham

This memorial sits on
the junction of the
old A77 (Ayr Road)
and Mearns Road.
Robert Pollok (1798-
1827) was a poet,
born near this spot
— his most famous
poem 'The Course of
Time' dealt with
man's religious
history. He died in
Southampton on his
way to a sanatorium
in Italy.

Rouken Glen Park
Giffnock

Until the late 19th century,
Rouken Glen was part of the
Crum estate, but the next
owner, Archibald Corbett MP,
donated the grounds and
mansion (demolished in 1963)
to the City of Glasgow in 1906.
The pond and boathouse,
pictured here, were opened in
1924. Today the park offers
many attractions including
woodland walks, a walled
garden, children's play areas,
Ranger services with guided
walks, cafés, putting, boating
and a garden centre.

Glasgow Royal Concert Hall
Sauchiehall Street

Designed by Sir Leslie Martin
and opened in October 1990 to
replace St Andrew's Hall,
Charing Cross, which was
destroyed by fire in 1962, the
Concert Hall sits at the junction
of Buchanan Street and
Sauchiehall Street. At the heart
of Scottish metropolitan life,
with two halls, the larger of
which seats 2500, this venue
hosts a wide range of concerts.
In front of the Concert Hall
stands a statue of Donald Dewar
(1937-2000), Scotland's
inaugural First Minister.

Royal Exchange Square
City Centre

This square, built around what is now the Gallery of Modern Art, dates from 1827 (Archibald Elliot II, David Hamilton and Robert Black), and was planned to a very high specification. At one time the square was the financial hub of the city. However, it is now renowned for its fashionable bars, restaurants and pavement cafés. Also of note, are the two highly decorated stone arches with Ionic columns adjoining a building with a magnificent Greek style, six-pillared portico — previously the Royal Bank of Scotland (now the rear entrance to Borders book store on Buchanan Street).

Ruchill Church Hall
Shakespeare Street

Completed in 1900, this Charles Rennie Mackintosh design was built as a mission hall for Westbourne Free Church (the neighbouring Ruchill Parish Church was not completed until 1905). Considered to be one of CRM's minor works, this white sandstone, two storey, Art Nouveau building has two halls and two committee rooms, all currently in use.

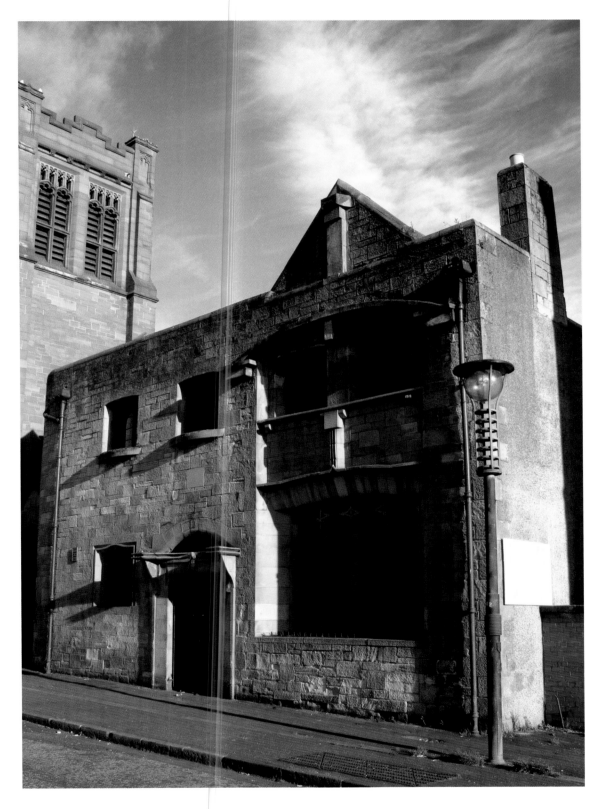

Rutherglen Town Hall
Main Street

Built in 1862, this Victorian
Town Hall was designed by
Charles Wilson. Rutherglen is
Scotland's oldest royal burgh,
lying two miles to the south-
east of the city centre. The
imposing building, with its
distinctive clock tower has
recently undergone a £10
million refurbishment, including
restoration of the Grand Hall.

**St Andrew's
Cathedral**
Clyde Street

Glasgow's Roman
Catholic cathedral
was the city's first
real attempt at
Gothic revivalism.
Completed as a
church in 1816
(J.J. Gillespie
Graham) at the then
huge cost of £16,000,
it went on to
become a cathedral
in 1889. The
building, overlooking
the Clyde, is flanked
by two octagonal
towers. Relatively
unadorned externally,
it has a handsome
plaster-vaulted
interior.

St Andrew's Parish Church
St Andrews Square

Sitting in its own square just south of
Glasgow Cross, this Georgian-towered
baroque temple was completed in 1759 by
Allan Dreghorn and Mungo Nasmith. The
finest church in Scotland of its time, its west
elevation is entirely taken up with a six
Corinthian-pillared portico. Above this there
is a pediment with Glasgow's Coat of Arms.
The magnificent tower, with a blue clock on
each of its four faces, is topped by a weather
vane. Internally, it is no less stunning.

St Mungo Museum of Religious Life and Art
Castle Street

In the shadow of Glasgow Cathedral, this building, in Scots Baronial style by Ian Begg, was completed in 1992. A major tourist attraction, the museum deals with the role of religion in people's lives across the world, with the six main religions explored: Buddhism, Christianity, Hinduism, Islam, Judaism and Sikhism. Amongst the artwork on display is 'Christ of St John of the Cross' by Salvador Dali. Outside is Britain's first permanent Zen Garden.

St Enoch Travel Centre
St Enoch Square

Originally St Enoch
Underground Station,
this is a pretty
Jacobean toy-like
structure by James
Miller (1896). It stands
in St Enoch Square,
which until 1977 was
dominated by St Enoch
Station and Hotel.
These were replaced in
1989 by the St Enoch
Centre, an enormous
glass-covered shopping
precinct.

**St George's Tron
Parish Church**
Nelson Mandela Place

By William Stark, 1809,
St George's stands at
the bottom of West
George Street in the
middle of what is now
Nelson Mandela Place
(previously St George's
Place). A well known
Glasgow landmark, this
rather squat church has
a tall, five-sectioned
Baroque-style clock
tower, topped by a
dome and an obelisk.
The four other obelisks
were originally to have
been statues.

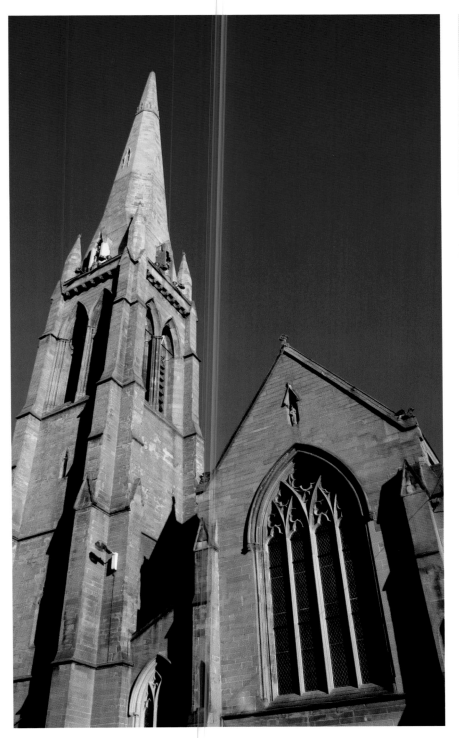

**St Stephen's
Renfield Church**
Bath Street

On the corner of
Holland Street stands
Bath Street's only
surviving steeple.
The graceful spire
adorns the church
built in 1852 by
J.T. Emmett. It was
Glasgow's first
example of
'Tractarian' Gothic,
and the first of many
of the city's tall
spires. The church
was saved from
demolition in 1960,
but in the process
lost many of its
sculptures.

St Vincent Place
City Centre

St Vincent Place lies
between George
Square and Buchanan
Street. This view
looking westwards
towards St Vincent
Street is dominated
by the former *Citizen*
newspaper offices
(1889) at 24 St
Vincent Place. This
richly adorned red
Dumfriesshire
sandstone building
has an arcaded attic
storey. Also in view
is the clock beneath
its octagonal turret.
The building has
been more recently
used by the Bank of
England.

St Vincent Street Church
St Vincent Street

Situated at the junction
of Pitt Street, the
St Vincent Street Free
Church of Scotland (1857-
59) by Alexander 'Greek'
Thompson, was the follow
up to his Caledonia Road
Church, and is now
considered to be one
of Glasgow's finest
buildings. The temple
itself has two grand
porticos on its north and
south façades, and stands
on a massive podium. The
tower, which can be seen
from George Square,
embraces Egyptian,
Assyrian, Indian and
Graeco-Roman styles.
The church's spectacular
interior was designed
to hold 1500 people.

Sauchiehall Street
City Centre

Sauchiehall Street is Glasgow's best known thoroughfare, stretching 2.5 km (1¼ miles) from Buchanan Street to Kelvingrove. In addition to being one of Glasgow's busiest shopping areas, fully pedestrianised and lined with trees at its eastern end, it offers many other attractions such as the McLellan Galleries, The Willow Tea Rooms (Charles Rennie Mackintosh), the Centre for Contemporary Arts and the Royal Concert Hall, all of which are open to the public. Sauchiehall Street is also renowned for its lively nightlife!

Sauchiehall Street
City Centre

Skypark
Elliot Place

Glasgow's state-of-the-art
landmark business complex in
the Finnieston area, has
attracted a wide range of
companies. Located on the
fringe of the West End, adjacent
to the Clydeside Expressway,
the multi-storey building,
primarily glass, is an excellent
example of 21st-century
contemporary architecture.

South Frederick Street
City Centre

This view northwards
up South Frederick
Street from Ingram
Street. The imposing
City Chambers are on
the right, with the
modern blocks
of the University of
Strathclyde in the
distance, beyond North
Frederick Street.

**South Portland Street
Suspension Bridge**
City Centre

This graceful, much
photographed footbridge
was designed by Alexander
Kirkland and built by
George Martin in 1853. It
crosses the Clyde from
Customs House Quay to
Carlton Place. The Greek
pylons with their triumphal
arches are linked by a 126m
(414 ft) span with red and
white wrought-iron
latticework. Pedestrians
were originally charged a
halfpenny to cross!

The Tall Ship
Yorkhill Quay

The three-masted SS *Glenlee* is one of only five 19th century Clyde-built sailing ships still afloat. She was built in 1896 in Port Glasgow, is 75m (245 ft) in length and weighs 1613 tons. Having had various names, including *Islamount*, *Clarastella* and *Galatea*, she was decommissioned in 1969, and purchased by the Clyde Maritime Trust in 1992. After much restoration work, she is now a floating museum with an adjoining visitor centre.

Templeton's Carpet Factory
Glasgow Green

John Templeton, the carpet manufacturer, had been operating a successful carpet factory here since 1856, but in 1888 needed to expand. He commissioned William Leiper to build the extension with an ornamental frontage facing Glasgow Green. Leiper based his design on the Doge's Palace in Venice, and the result was a masterpiece in red brickwork, using glazed, unglazed and coloured bricks producing a fascinating shimmering mosaic. The ornate sandstone centre section is topped by a statue of St Enoch. Carpets are no longer made here, but the façade remains 'the world's finest example of decorative brickwork'.

Tolbooth Steeple
Glasgow Cross

The dominating feature of Glasgow Cross, the Tolbooth Steeple is all that remains of the New Tolbooth or Town House dating back to 1626 (John Boyd). The seven-storey, 38m (126ft) tower now stands in splendid isolation at what was once the hub of Glasgow's old city centre. Above the blue and gold clocks on each of its four sides sits a crown topped by a weather vane.

Trades House
Glassford Street

Completed in 1794 by Robert Adam, this is his sole surviving work in Glasgow. The Trades House was intended as a meeting place for the city's tradesmen, and indeed continues to be, making it the second-oldest public building in Glasgow still used for its original intention, the Cathedral being the oldest. The beautiful symmetry is best appreciated from Garth Street — an Ionic centrepiece raised on a plinth and topped by a dome. At the base of the flagstaff is a carving of the city's Coat of Arms flanked by two female figures.

Trinity College
Lynedoch Street

The four towers situated within the Park area are such a distinctive feature of the Glasgow skyline. Three of them belong to the former Trinity College (the other being the white tower of Park Church), the tallest of which has a balcony. This college was completed in 1861 by Charles Wilson as the Free Church College, and renamed Trinity in 1929, until closure in the 1970s. The entire block has now been converted into flats and offices.

Tron Steeple
Trongate

Straddling the Trongate's southern pavement, this impressive clock tower is all that remains of the 15th-century Church of St Mary, destroyed by fire in 1793. The steeple, a sturdy four stage structure with Gothic windows and heavy Scots spire, actually dates from 1631, and the arches were constructed in 1855 by John Carrick. Nearby is the replacement church by James Adam (1794) which is now the Tron Theatre. Below the clock on its western face is an interesting interpretation of the city's Coat of Arms.

Turnberry House
Hope Street

On the corner of Hope
Street and West George
Street stands J.A.
Campbell's 1903 master-
piece — a red sandstone
Spanish renaissance
alcázar covering eight
storeys. Although plain
in design up to the
seventh floor, a two
storey arcade then rises
from a balcony to the
cornice. This building is
now used as office
accommodation for
several companies.

UGC Cinema
Renfrew Street

The UGC Cinema is a recent addition to
Glasgow's skyline in the heart of the city centre,
at the junction of West Nile Street and Renfrew
Street. Completed in 2001, this ultra-modern
building covers six floors, and is the world's
tallest cinema! Films are shown throughout the
day and night on its 18 screens.

University of Glasgow
Gilmorehill

Founded in the mid-15th-century, the university was located in the city centre at High Street until 1870. Today, most of the university's departments are on the Gilmorehill campus, grouped around the neo-Gothic main building by Sir George Gilbert Scott (1870). The tower, which is 54m (177 ft), was added in 1884 by Sir George's son, John, and has become one of Glasgow's most familiar landmarks. The Lion and Unicorn staircase was moved stone by stone from the previous site at High Street. The university, today is a renowned worldwide institution with around 20,000 students.

Victoria Bridge
City Centre

Spanning the Clyde between Gorbals and Bridgegate, Victoria Bridge is the oldest Clyde bridge in the city. There has been a crossing point here since the 14th century, but this structure dates from 1854 (James Walker). Considered to be Glasgow's finest bridge, its graceful five arches are of Kingston granite.

Virginia Place
Merchant City

The name Virginia recalls the times of Glasgow's tobacco trade of the 18th century. Originally, the Virginia Mansion was designed to close the vista of Virginia Street. However, the Mansion, in Virginia Place, was converted by David Hamilton in 1841 to the (former) Union Bank which continued with the role of closing the street. The structure that now exists at this spot is an attractive single storey domed hall by James Salmon (1853), with a south facing façade displaying French detail and sculptures.

West George Street
Merchant City
NS587656

Running from George Square westwards past Blythswood Square, the street was originally known as Camperdown Place after the great naval victory. West George Street has many fine Victorian buildings in its lower section. This view, however, is typical of the upper section and is taken from Blythswood Square showing the fine terraces of two to three storey 19th-century houses and offices.

Willow Tea Rooms
Sauchiehall Street

This building was the last of four 'temples to temperance' designed by Charles Rennie Mackintosh for Kate Cranston in 1904. Now partly hidden behind the trees of the pedestrianised Sauchiehall Street, the tall, slender, white façade is a delight. A jewellery shop occupies the ground floor, but tea and light meals are still served in the Room de Luxe and on The Gallery, where many of CRMs decorative charms remain.

Woodlands Terrace
Park District

Woodlands Terrace lies
on the southern fringe
of the 19th-century
Park development laid
out by Charles Wilson
between 1855-63.
However, the architect
for the majority of
Woodlands Terrace was
John Baird — his
classical style is well
displayed in the
porticos of the three
storey terraced
houses.